FROM THE VINE
Exploring Michigan Wineries

SHARON KEGERREIS AND LORRI HATHAWAY

ANN ARBOR
MEDIA GROUP

Ann Arbor Media Group LLC
2500 S. State Street
Ann Arbor, MI 48104

Printed and bound in China.
10 9 8 7 6 5 4 3 2

Library of Congress Cataloging-in-Publication Data

Kegerreis, Sharon, 1968-
From the vine : exploring Michigan wineries / Sharon Kegerreis and Lorri Hathaway.
p. cm.
Includes bibliographical references.
ISBN-13: 978-1-58726-460-3 (hardcover : alk. paper)
ISBN-10: 1-58726-460-9 (hardcover : alk. paper)
1. Wine and wine making--Michigan. 2. Wineries--Michigan. I. Hathaway, Lorri, 1969- II. Title.

TP557.K44 2007
641.2'209774--dc22
2007004994

Designed by Somberg Design, Ann Arbor, Michigan.
www.sombergdesign.com

Foreword

The unique beauty of Michigan's two peninsulas is surrounded by 3,200 miles of fresh water. More than 100 historic lighthouses dot the picturesque Great Lakes shoreline where treasured Petoskey stones are often uncovered. Inland, more than 11,000 lakes and rivers mark our rolling countryside and wind through our dense forests of sky-high pines, maples and spruces.

Our Great Lakes state is also home to acres of fields and orchards bearing apples, cherries, blueberries, and deliciously diverse fruit and vegetable crops. A notable fruit growing on more than 13,000 acres of hillsides are grapes for jams, jellies, grape juice, and one of Michigan's fastest growing industries—wine.

On the pages of *From the Vine,* you'll discover the individual personalities of our winemakers—people dedicated to bringing you fine wines with character and flavor that reflect our unique Great Lakes' growing conditions and soils. These wines are standouts at national and international competitions, winning awards against wines from renowned winemaking regions worldwide. Expect to be delighted—and surprised—by the world-class wines being produced in Michigan.

It's time to explore Michigan by taking an enjoyable journey into our celebrated wine country. Learn what to expect and what not to miss and meet those who are sculpting new territory with their wines. Then plan your getaway to our eclectic and award-winning wineries, glorious vineyards, and unbeatable natural wonders to create your own memories along the trail.

Governor Jennifer Granholm

Contents

Introduction

It's time to take another look at Michigan wine. Fifty wineries stretching throughout every corner of our "mitten" state and into the Upper Peninsula are producing very dry to very sweet wines, many of which are beating wines from renowned wine regions, like California and New York, in national and international competitions, year after year.

"All wines are local wines somewhere. Taste with an open mind. We honor the cranberry wine drinkers as well as the Pinot Noir drinkers. There are no shoulds or shouldn'ts here. Come celebrate with us."
—RICK MOERSCH, VINTNER, ROUND BARN WINERY.

Appreciate Michigan wines just as you may appreciate wines from other parts of the world. If you're new to wine, visiting our Great Lakes state wineries is a perfectly comfortable way to find a wine to love. Believe us, the wines are so diverse, from one end of the spectrum to the other, that you will fall in love with Michigan all over again because of the great wines being produced here.

And, yes, there are the sweet cherry and apple wines and hybrid wines with quirky names you may never have heard of, like Maréchal Foch and Vignoles.

Traditional European vinifera grapes, such as Cabernet Franc, Pinot Grigio, Chardonnay, and Pinot Noir that are producing some of the finest wines in the world, are also grown in Michigan.

Indeed, in many of our stories, we share medals won at prestigious competitions and identify wines offered at each winery. It would be nearly impossible, though, to list all of the awards won by wineries in our state and all their wines. We'd fill up our book with award and wine lists! Rather, our stories give insight into the people behind Michigan wine and give you a behind-the-scenes peek into their winemaking operations. And like us, you'll discover Michigan wineries are run by farmers, entrepreneurs, and conservationists, all rolled into one.

These men and women of Michigan wine are passionate for preserving our farmland and for growing high-quality fruit. They are passionate for sharing how best to enjoy their wines and appreciate the flavors that are truly unique to Michigan for its maritime Great Lakes climate. In essence, they are passionate for creating value-added agriculture and destinations where great wines and food are married for the ultimate experience.

"It's like Tara in Gone with the Wind ... *it's the land. Mother Nature either shines on you or she doesn't. When everything connects, it's just astounding."*
—DR. ROBERTA KUNTZ, VINTNER, CHATEAU DE LEELANAU

Noteworthy, Michigan is located on the same latitudes as the world-renowned wine regions of Europe. Our cooler climate is consistent with that in Bordeaux, France, and the Rhine region of Germany, for instance. The exceptional growing conditions provide us with wines that match the best wines in the world while offering a uniqueness just to Michigan.

One of the themes we heard often during our vineyard chats is that wines are grown from the ground. Yes, *wines* are grown from the ground. The terrain, or terroir in wine industry terms, is either ideal for growing grapes, or it isn't. The vines are nurtured by hand and grapes are largely handpicked with bigger wineries using specialized, very expensive equipment to assist with crops. Either way, the winemakers are in their vineyards and working closely with other growers to ensure vines are balanced perfectly with fruit—and each vine is unique, as we learned from Lee Lutes, the winemaker for Black Star Farms.

Each year brings a new challenge, or mighty triumph as the 2005 vintage did. It has been claimed as the best season for producing outstanding red wines. Lee also gives the tip to think of vintages as a year in your life. What memory can be recalled with a yummy 2005 Pinot Noir? For us, it was the year we went into high gear to bring this book to you.

Our land is so diverse; a Riesling at one winery may taste vastly different from a Riesling grown a few miles down the road. Compare the wines from winery to winery, as you'll likely find a favorite wine in your preferred style.

One of our favorite quotes within these pages reiterates these differences. Eddie O'Keefe III, of Chateau Grand Traverse, northern Michigan's first winery, shares, "A sweet and complex Riesling wine is much like dressing up in a snowmobile suit, whereas a dry Riesling wine is more revealing, much like standing there naked." We believe you'll enjoy the original, personable quotes throughout our stories.

"Yes, there's a technique to enjoying a good glass of wine. The most important thing, though? Simply enjoying it; if you like it, drink it."
—JOHN BURTKA, VINTNER, CHERRY CREEK CELLARS

A broad smile, work jeans, and, in harvest, red-stained hands are the attire of the winemakers. They work hard, and when Mother Nature and the Great Lakes climate cooperate and the fruit is the best it can be, they are deeply rewarded with fine wines that make it to your dinner table.

Meet the hardworking winemakers within these pages, and then go to their tasting rooms where you'll meet many of them pouring their wines. You'll be encouraged to drink whatever you like. We encourage you to buy what you like in return for the opportunity to sample wines.

"The water is the reason fruit grows here. Water is the reason we're here and why others come here."
—BOB JACOBSON, PROPRIETOR, LEELANAU WINE CELLARS

It is important to note that we are not wine experts. Our shared backgrounds of growing up in northern Michigan lake communities of Leelanau Peninsula and Charlevoix, traveling our nation and the world, and settling in southern Michigan in East Lansing and Chelsea, have ignited a new appreciation for "all things Michigan" and, in particular, Michigan wine.

Evidence of our passion is the launch of our company, Michigan Vine, in 2003, exclusively devoted to promoting Michigan wine. We chucked corporate careers in favor of more time at the lake, casual workdays visiting the wineries, and writing from the comfort of our homes. Our philosophy is shared with winegrower Spencer Stegenga of Bowers Harbor who says, "We just want to have fun with the lifestyle."

So plan your "girls only" play day, or escape to Michigan wine country for a romantic getaway. Get married in the vineyard, or celebrate your fiftieth anniversary in style. Or, for no occasion at all, spend a lazy Saturday touring a wine trail.

Read on to meet the winemakers and then visit them to experience their wine and immerse yourself in the vines.

A TOAST
(WITH MICHIGAN WINE, OF COURSE)!

Lake Michigan Shore Wine Trail

LAKE MICHIGAN SHORE AND FENNVILLE AVAS

The Lake Michigan Shore viticultural area, with its blend of northern continental and maritime climates, produces distinctive fruit-forward wines of unparalleled quality. The region hugs the southeast shore of Lake Michigan, extending from the Michigan-Indiana border north 70 miles to the Kalamazoo River at Saugatuck. Wines grown at the southern end have a noticeably lower acidity than the more minerally wines from the northern extreme, and the ability to ripen long-season reds tends to diminish as one progresses from south to north.

Overall, the long growing season, with its cool ripening period during the last 60 days, results in wines having an intense fruit character not found in very many wine-growing regions. Even the flagship red wines, like Pinot Noir and Cabernet Franc, have a distinctive fruit-forward character that is not commonly found in warmer areas. The firm acidity of the white wines and the mild-mannered tannins of the red wines, along with the distinctive fruit character, make Lake Michigan Shore wines very "food-friendly" and "European" in character.

—DOUG WELSCH, VINTNER,
FENN VALLEY VINEYARDS

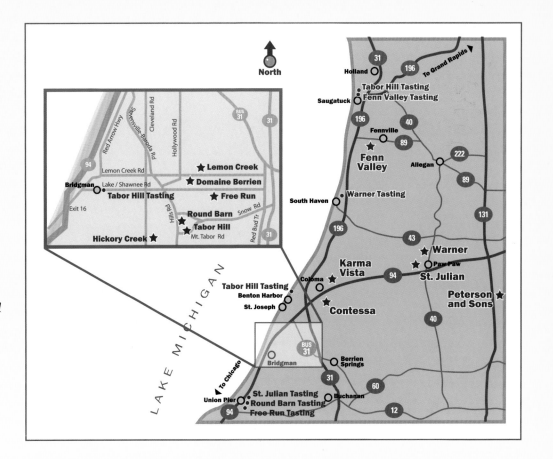

Contessa Wine Cellars

A subtle, yet distinct difference you may note when visiting Contessa Wine Cellars is sipping wine in elegant sheer-rim crystal glasses appropriate for enjoying wine to its fullest potential. Tony and Liz Peterson, proprietors of the winery, wouldn't have you taste their wines any other way.

The German-crafted Stölzle stemware, Tony states, has a huge impact on how his wines are perceived. "First impressions are everything," Tony strongly believes. In a taste test, using regular wine glasses with a fuller lip, we were surprised at the difference.

Making wine since age 12 as an apprentice to his father, Duane Peterson of Peterson and Sons Natural Wine, Tony learned the trade hands-on. "I cut, crushed, bottled, and labeled," Tony recalls. It wasn't until after college that his passion for winemaking took hold—and took off. Tony and Liz sold everything to build their dream tasting room atop the hills of Coloma and open their winery in 2002.

The European-style, A-frame tasting room is fronted with tall windows that open to an outdoor patio and overlook apple trees and vines growing Merlot and Pinot Grigio grapes. Inside, you'll quickly glance up at the spirited portrait of Liz, painted by her mother years before and the inspiration behind the wine labels.

Liz's great-grandmother's chair sits adjacent to a stately grand piano and is positioned to face the gleaming mahogany, cherry, and oak wine bar hand-made by Liz's father. "We like to think of her in her chair, encouraging us with her spirit," Tony reflects. Contessa Wine Cellars is named for Liz's mother's maiden name.

The Italian influence continues in the naming of wines. You'll love Bianco Bello, meaning "lovely white," a semisweet, smooth French-American blend with floral tones, and Rosa d'amore, translated to "rose of love" from Italian. This garnet-rich, dry wine is nicely balanced and, Tony shares, "perfect with meals and chocolate."

The winery produces a "Michigan Merlot" that Tony describes as a "full-bodied red," aged in French oak for 18 months. The Merlot is one of our favorites, as is his Pinot Grigio, a dry wine that is crisp and light. A visitor favorite is the heavenly Black Raspberry dessert wine that is surprisingly dry and simply delicious with no sulfites added. Don't be surprised if this wine isn't available during a visit, as it sells out quickly.

Dangling, fanciful, grape-detailed chandeliers reflect the natural light pouring in through the expansive windows, and comfortable stools invite you to relax and savor the wines. The ambience is relaxed and completely unpretentious.

Top off your visit with a purchase of a cheese-and-cracker plate and a bottle of wine to enjoy on the outdoor patio, followed up by a visit to the Chocolate Garden. Chocolatier Tina Buck hand rolls chocolate truffles, including one infused with Contessa's Lago Rosso. The truffles are truly divine, especially when paired with a glass of Contessa's Rosa d'amore.

GET IN TOUCH

3235 Friday Road
Coloma
(269) 468-5534
winemaker@contessawinecellars.com
www.contessawinecellars.com
GPS: N 42° 10.23102, W 086° 18.3843

The Chocolate Garden

Sink your teeth into the round, flavor-rich truffles sure to surprise any chocolate lover.

Creating a buzz along the Lake Michigan Shore Wine Trail is The Chocolate Garden. Chocolatier Tina Buck hand makes chocolate truffles unlike any we've tasted. Sink your teeth into the round, flavor-rich truffles sure to surprise any chocolate lover. These truffles are creamy and sumptuous without an outer shell.

Truffles are rolled in coarse chocolate with various accents. Among the favorites are the Solera Cream Double Gold, made with St. Julian's Solera Cream Sherry, and Lago Rosso, made with Contessa Wine Cellars' red wine. These wine-infused truffles are sensuously mouthwatering. Follow our lead and stock up on truffles when you visit.

The Chocolate Garden is located in a charming, mint-colored cottage surrounded by peach trees. The nearly 145-year-old Italianate farmhouse, next to the retail store, adds to the romantic setting just minutes off the busy highway. Located just half a mile south of Contessa Wine Cellars at the Coloma exit, with Karma Vista Vineyards to the north, the charming chocolate shop is a perfect accompaniment to Michigan wine.

GET IN TOUCH

2691 Friday Road
Coloma
(269) 468-9866
tina@chocolategarden.com
www.chocolategarden.com
GPS: N 42°9.65892, W 086°18.42414

Domaine Berrien Cellars

Special order large bottles of wine.

Wines influenced by those grown in the Rhône Valley in France, and other renowned wine-growing regions in Europe, can be enjoyed with a picnic lunch in Domaine Berrien's vineyard. Pair goodies with what is believed to be Michigan's first locally produced Syrah and Marsanne, a lovely white native to the Rhône. Winemaker Wally Maurer enjoys your questions, so make the time to learn why Wally's part-time hobby turned into a full-time passion.

"It was a gradual interest that grew out of control," says wife Katie Maurer, winery proprietor with Wally and a civil engineer by training. Wally started making batches of wine in the basement with his late father-in-law, Tom Fricke, for friends and family as a hobby. One of Tom's original blends made since the early 1970s is Wolf's Prairie Red. The De Chaunac and Chelois blend remains a staple among the Maurers' wine offerings. They boldly promote the wine with "This wolf can make you howl." We admit to being part of the pack of fans who love this wine.

Tom first planted vines on a small farm in 1970 to grow grapes for their hobby wine venture. The vision kept growing and, in 1990, Domaine Berrien's 80-acre farm in Michigan's most dense fruit farm county, Berrien County, was established. In 2001, Wally decided it was time to turn his hobby into a full-time business. "We were making varietally correct wines from estate-grown Michigan fruit, and the wines shone in blind tastings. We wanted to be able to sell it."

Wally confesses to his tastes maturing over the years and finds himself making wines he and Katie prefer to drink. "We love wines from the Rhône region of France. We really enjoy how they taste on our palates. We kept saying, 'we can do this.'" Wally believes that they were the first in Michigan to plant Syrah, Viognier, and Marsanne, varietals from the Rhône, leading the region's growth in these varieties.

Wally's 2005 Marsanne took golds at the Great Lakes Wine Competition and Michigan Wine and Spirits Competition with his fifth commercial vintage. "I make an 'Hermitage Blanc' style Marsanne, which is 15 percent Rousanne and the remainder Marsanne. Hermitage Blanc is also from the Rhône. Marsanne so far has been winter hearty. It sprouts later in the spring, which protects it from late frost damage. Its success has driven me to plant more vines to sell to smaller wineries in the southwest region." He also grows and sells his Riesling grapes with the possibility to make a Riesling of his own in the future.

Twenty-seven acres of grape varietals are grown in vineyards affectionately named Katherine's Vineyard, Abigail's Vineyard, and Martha's Vineyard, after Katie, her mother, and her grandmother, respectively. The Maurers continually increase their acreage of grapevines to try to keep up with demand.

"We try to plant two acres of new vines every spring so we're not running out of everything so fast," says Katie. Merlot, Lemberger, and Pinot Grigio also grow on their estate, although Wally loves to talk up the Pinot Noir. "It is the right grape for Michigan. It grows beautifully here." Their 2005 Traminette, a Seyval-Gewürztraminer hybrid blend with spicy aromas, and 2005 Pinot Grigio are also worthy of talk, winning golds at the Great Lakes Wine Competition, and double gold at the Michigan Wine and Spirits Competition for the 2005 Traminette.

One wine they are passionate about selling is their Cabernet Franc, a favorite of Wally's mom Kathleen Maurer who lost her fight to breast cancer. Kathleen sometimes sipped her favorite wine as a way to relax from her active career in real estate, where she also proudly gave the wine as a housewarming gift to clients. Not only will you enjoy the smooth, French-style red wine, you will also be helping a good cause as the Maurers donate $1.00 to the Breast Cancer Research Foundation from every bottle of Cabernet Franc sold, in honor of Kathleen.

"We want to

share our love

for the wines."

GET IN TOUCH

398 East Lemon Creek Road
Berrien Springs
(269) 473-9463
winery@domaineberrien.com
www.domaineberrien.com
GPS: N 41° 57.43722, W 086° 26.94792

Other favorites include Steelhead White, named for the trout swimming in nearby St. Joseph River, a dry blend of Seyval Blanc, Chardonnay, and Pinot Grigio with hints of citrus, and St. Vincent, named for the patron saint of wine grape growers, a mellow, light-bodied red.

"We make an authentic Bordeaux style wine—our Crown of Cab," says Wally. "It's the crown jewel of our cellar." It's aged for 24 months and is a wonderfully smooth-tasting blend of Cabernet Franc, Merlot, and Cabernet Sauvignon.

Plan an extended visit at Domaine Berrien, as you'll likely find Wally and Katie behind the tasting bar pouring their wines and sharing tips on how best to enjoy each wine. You may also be warmly greeted by Baco Noir, the Maurers' black Lab. "He loves to play with kids who visit the tasting room while their parents sip wine," shares Katie. Spend time asking Wally questions; he is happy to take the mystery out of wine. "We want you to come in, ask questions, and get comfortable," says Wally. "We want to share our love for the wines."

You're invited to reserve a picnic table in advance by phoning ahead. Take along a loaded picnic basket for a casual lunch in the vineyard, or stock up on gourmet fare available for purchase in the tasting room. Pack your picnic basket full of locally crafted cheese and sausage, wild Alaskan salmon, bruschetta and tampenades, and surround yourself with flowing grapevines.

Syrah vs. Shiraz:
What's the Difference?

As Syrah vines are expanding through the Lake Michigan Shore Wine Trail, a common question is "What's the difference between Syrah and Shiraz?" The two are actually different names for the same red grape. When grown in the United States, France, and many other countries, it is most commonly referred to as Syrah, whereas in Australia and South Africa it is called Shiraz. However, as Australians have made "Shiraz" famous, some American winemakers who are crafting Australian-style wine from the grape are now calling it Shiraz.

Syrah, as we call it, is a red grape that produces a complex, spicy wine with hints of blackberry, plum, and pepper. As different temperatures affect the outcome of the Syrah, be sure to sample the unique Syrah flavors being grown in Michigan's cool climate.

Fenn Valley Vineyards

Fenn Valley Vineyards is a destination winery on Michigan's sunset side, just a few miles in from Lake Michigan's shoreline. The only winery in the Fennville appellation offers award-winning wines and fun opportunities for learning more about wine during vineyard and cellar tours and winemaking dinners, designed for everyone from the first-time taster to the wine enthusiast.

A quest to find the perfect growing conditions for their vineyard landed the Chicago-native Welsch family in Fennville, just five miles east of Lake Michigan. "I was just finishing college, and my dad wanted to go into farming," remembers Doug Welsch, winemaker and proprietor of Fenn Valley Vineyards.

It was important to Doug and his father, William Welsch, that they select the most desirable site to grow premium wine grapes. They traveled to Finger Lakes and talked with growers and visited several properties throughout Illinois, Wisconsin, Indiana, and Michigan before selecting the 230-acre farm. "It was not an accident that we selected this property," shares Doug, "It was a researched effort."

William took a short growing course at Ohio State University and talked to local growers before planting the first vines in 1973 into the deep, sandy soils of their new property. The cool, moderating climate of nearby Lake Michigan provides a great benefit to the vines, allowing the fruit to thrive. Indeed, the area has the distinct honor of being Michigan's first recognized appellation in 1981, called Fennville AVA.

Doug's 230-acre farm includes 52 acres of flourishing grapevines, mostly consisting of 10 proven varietals in the region. To keep up with demand, Doug is testing new varietals and plans to add more vines in the near future.

To capture the character of the Great Lakes region in every bottle, Doug carefully attends each vine. At the peak of ripeness, the grapes are harvested and crafted into wine in the underground cellar. An artful balance of old-world techniques and modern technology has earned Doug more than 200 awards for his wine, including his Riesling, which won double gold medals at the Michigan State Wine and Spirits Competition.

The expansive tasting room sits amidst the vineyard and features red brick archways leading to custom-built, recessed wine racks accented by rock and timber pillars. Make your way up to the large U-shaped bar area to sample wines.

A must to taste is Doug's most popular red Capriccio, a big, soft red wine that balances fruitiness and dryness, which has won Best of Show at the Michigan State Fair, and is one of our favorites. More big reds include the winery's barrel-aged Chancellor and Meritage, a Bordeaux-style blend of Cabernet Franc, Cabernet Sauvignon, and Merlot.

Their most popular white, Lakeshore Demi-Sec, is a German-style wine bursting with floral and apple fruit character. You may also enjoy the Chardonel, a complex, crisp white wine hybrid that is a cross of Chardonnay and Seyval grapes. Doug's elegant Pinot Grigio is another one of our favorites to take home.

Sample directly from the tanks and barrels during Doug's popular cellar tours, but be sure to reserve your spot ahead of time as these tours are almost always sold out. Sign up for a wagon-ride tour through the vineyard, where Doug shares his winemaking process, from vine to wine, and his teaching skills come to life. Glorious autumn colors envelop you as you taste small samples of wine during your tour and unwind amongst the vines.

"We show wines in the fashion they are supposed to be—with food…"

An event not to miss is the Annual Pre-Release Barrel Tasting where you will taste six wines that represent their best varieties. "You get to taste the wines before they're bottled," explains Doug. Experience the wines and learn about them firsthand as Doug explains the vintage. The wines are brought out one by one and typically include two reds, two dry whites, and two additional whites of some type. During the event, you will also be able to pre-order the wine at their highest discount, usually 25 to 30 percent off.

Take a lunch or snack to enjoy at one of the picnic tables under a vine-covered portico, and sip a glass of wine within view of the vineyards. Reserve the patio in advance, fire up the outdoor grill for roasting your meats and vegetables, and buy a bottle or two of wine to enjoy for a fun afternoon in the vineyard with family and friends.

Sign up very early for Doug's always-sold-out winemaker's dinner to enjoy five or six glasses of wine paired with gourmet fare prepared by a local chef. Or join in on the annual "chili cook-off and wine lover's potluck." This fun winter event gives you the chance to show off your favorite chili and side dish recipes.

"We show wines in the fashion they are supposed to be—with food," says Doug.

American Viticulture Appellation (AVA)

An American Viticulture Appellation (AVA) is a government-approved geographical region under which a winegrower is authorized to identify and market wine. AVAs define and protect geographically named wines, spirits, and even some foods. The Great Lakes have had a positive impact on Michigan's ability to grow quality grapes along the lakeshore with climate and soil varying dramatically by region. Combined with established tourism areas, regions in Michigan that have earned the official AVA designation include Lake Michigan Shore, Fennville, Leelanau Peninsula, and Old Mission Peninsula.

Free Run Cellars

Wind your way through fertile grapevine-covered countryside to Free Run Cellars to find creative wines atypical to the region. Muscat Ottonel, a fruity dry wine that flairs with a bit of spice, is the winery's showpiece, as are Syrah and Mezzo, a blend of Gewürztraminer and Traminette.

Free spirits Matt Moersch and Chris Moersch are the driving force behind this wine venture. The brothers were bred to be winemakers, working in vineyards since they were young alongside their father, Rick Moersch, proprietor of Round Barn Winery. Their proud dad jokes about his sons need to do their own experimenting and produce wines that interest them. "The animals were getting restless. When that happens, you put them in a bigger pasture."

The new generation of the Moersch legacy is making strides in producing notable Michigan wine and further solidifying the Moersch name in Michigan's wine history.

"We really enjoy doing small batches of single vineyard wines," explains Chris, General Manager of Free Run Cellars, as well as of Round Barn Winery. Chris further clarifies that rather than making wines from grapes pulled from multiple vineyard sites, they are capturing the unique flavors found within a single vineyard site.

Two thousand Pinot Gris vines were staked into the ground by the Free Run proprietors over long, 16-hour days. "There's a demand for Pinot Gris and it has shown excellent quality when grown in this area," reveals Matt.

The brothers also love a challenge. Matt shares, "Syrah is a very sensitive grape; it has to go in the best vineyard sites." Chris adds that, "Frankly, it would be nice having prime growing conditions for Syrah, without early frost and a bunch of rain. With the advent of global warming, it will flourish in the next 20 years." Until then, they have Michigan's inclement weather to contend with in producing their wines, although buying grapes from 40 acres of vineyard sites in the Lake Michigan Shore Appellation gives them flexibility.

Chris and Matt love their customers' reaction to finding Syrah on their wine list. "Their eyes just light up; they're so excited to find this wine in Michigan."

Our eyes notably brightened as well when we saw Syrah on their wine list; it's a favorite red wine we enjoy in the autumn and on cool, winter nights.

The winery's first vintage of Muscat Ottonel was produced using the Frizzante technique, which requires seven pounds of pressure to achieve the wine's "lightly sparkling" pizzazz that is generated after a second in-the-tank fermentation is interrupted. In Italian, Frizzante refers to wines with light effervescence, whereas Spumante indicates a sparkling wine.

"In the first release, about one in every six bottles met the Frizzante standard." Notably, their Muscat Ottonel in the Frizzante style earned a silver medal

For those who love traditional wines, you'll enjoy the dry

Gewürztraminer and a cherry wine…

Matt stretches the newly planted Pinot Gris vine.

at its first competition, the Michigan Wine and Spirits Competition. Chris shares they may tackle the Frizzante style again in the future using the fermentation tanks for crafting microbrews for Round Barn Winery. For now, Chris and Matt enjoy making a more traditional Muscat Ottonel; their "free spirit" method of winemaking is to make changes whenever they choose.

The term free run has two distinct meanings. At Free Run Cellars, the meaning is the free reign to be creative with selected grapes and in crafting small lots of wine, including an ice wine using Vidal Blanc grapes from a vineyard just down the road. Free run in relation to wine is the juice from the grapes that runs off naturally without any pressing. Free Run Cellars is the outlet where they have returned to small batch production.

One example of a unique wine they can produce again is Scheurebe, a wine produced 10 years ago with their father. Scheurebe is from Germany and is a cross of Riesling and Sylvaner; it makes a crisp, lively, and fruity wine. You may just find it on their wine list in the future.

For those who love traditional wines, you'll enjoy the dry Gewürztraminer and a cherry wine, made with Balaton® cherries from Hungary brought into

the United States for its unique taste and quality. Matt explains, "The difference in the Balaton cherry is that it is a balance between sweet and tart cherries; it has great flavor without being too sweet or too sour."

They also released a dry rosé made from a blend of Pinot Noir and Pinot Meunier grapes. "It's similar to a sparkling rosé without the sparkle," shares Matt.

Blending traditional grape varietals gives them freedom to experiment, although they are focused on crafting artisan wines with Alsatian flair. The Alsace region of France shares some similarities with Berrien County, such as climate, although the soil is very different. Chris explains, "Our sandy loam soils push fruit forward, so our styles of wine have bright fruit characteristics."

An Alsatian-style dry Riesling is one of Free Run Cellars' newer releases. Expect a crisp, dry wine with "a little bit of sweetness and acidity" to aid in the aging potential of the wine. Chris encourages enjoying the winery's new dry Riesling immediately, or cellaring it for three-to-five years for a more balanced finish.

In 2007, the Moersches renovated their wide-open garage into a relaxing and scenic tasting room.

French doors and glass windows provide an almost endless view of the vineyard. A small patio with tables and chairs provides a place for unwinding. The lovely, arrowhead-shaped pond that was added to their 10-acre property by the previous owner provides a peaceful, partially shady area for a vineyard picnic.

The intimate Free Run Cellars experience is distinctly different from the bustling activity you'll find at Round Barn Winery around a few country road bends. The heritage, though, is clear. The passion for enjoying great wine and creative winemaking was ignited while Chris and Matt ran through vineyards as children and learned to farm and care for the land under their dad's tutelage. From their mom, Sherrie, a former city girl who taught for 32 years, they learned to support one another's dreams.

The new generation of Moersches is proud of their upbringing and the unbreakable connection. "We're focused on precise growing processes and on clearly communicating our winemaking legacy," Chris concludes.

Just a few months after they officially opened in 2006, the Moersch brothers shared that they were kicking back one evening with a glass of wine when they looked at each other and, in awe, shouted, "We have a winery!"

GET IN TOUCH:

10062 Burgoyne Road
Berrien Springs
(269) 471-1737
info@freeruncellars.com
www.freeruncellars.com
GPS: N 41° 56.2419, W 086° 25.06848

Tasting Room:
Union Pier
9185 Union Pier Road
(269) 469-9443
GPS: N 41° 49.68822, W 086° 40.683

Hickory Creek Winery

Mike and Gottfried break from a busy harvest.

Dry wines rule here. The proprietors—an American, a German, and an Australian—wouldn't have it any other way. Wines influenced by the Hickory Creek team's diverse upbringings are presented in elegant, simple bottles. The wines have distinct flavors, including a vibrant Chardonnay, a versatile Cabernet Rosé, and a big, bold Shiraz.

Hickory Creek's other bold stance is to produce only European vinifera wines. This means that hybrid wines commonly grown in Michigan because of their cold-climate hardiness won't make the wine list. Rather, you'll see more traditional wines, including Riesling, Cabernet Franc, and Pinot Noir.

"We definitely don't fit everyone's tastes," agrees Mike De Schaaf, the American winemaker. "We decided to make the wines we like in the style we enjoy. All our wines are dry, except Apple, which has very little residual sugar."

Mike is the proprietor you'll run into most often. He is devoted to making the wine, managing the vine- yards where their fruit is grown, and working the tasting room outside of harvest season. He's also the one who won't let weeds get to his vines. "I don't like 'em," he confesses. Mike believes his grapes can be healthier and of higher quality if they are not fighting for nutrients with the weeds.

In addition, Mike continues to run his vineyard con- sulting company, which he started after departing from Round Barn Winery. At Round Barn Winery, he learned every aspect of the winemaking business, working as a winemaker for six of the nine years under skilled wine pro Rick Moersch.

In his favorite ripped work jeans, on his work truck, Mike shared why the winery's Cabernet Rosé can't be beat as an everyday wine to enjoy. "It's pink with a full body; it'll stand up to anything on the grill as it's so versatile," he touts. "It has wild berry fruits and smoky tarragon flavors."

Mike explained that rosés are very popular in France for the wine's lighter flavor and pink tones perfect for summer. The process to get a rosé enriches the texture of the wine and increases the density of the grape. "I bleed off a portion of the juice from the grape skins before fermentation and treat it like a white. This increases the skin-to-juice ratio of the red grape," Mike further explains. At the time of our visit, he had 12 barrels full of a Bordeaux blend, 60 percent of which was Cabernet Franc, waiting to be processed.

A typical day during harvest includes processing four tons of Riesling and late-night bottling of Late Harvest Riesling—mostly all done by the on-site winemaker. The Hickory Creek team plans to keep their operation small for the time being, wishing to make your experience personal when tasting their wines. "We always want at least one of us pouring the wines," Mike says.

Wine is created and served in an attractive, red barn built by the Australian, David Leslie, on his 40-acre property. David lives in Connecticut full-time with his family, after transferring there from Chicago with General Electric. David's parcel falls just short of Hickory Creek that runs east and west alongside the

tree line of the property; five acres of grapevines are planted in the front of the property, stretching alongside your drive up to the tasting room.

The German, Gottfried Hart, who is another proprietor you may run into on the weekends and, most definitely, during harvest, has an additional two acres on his property between Three Oaks and New Buffalo. Mike planted Pinot Gris vines on his farm down the road. They also buy grapes from clients of Mike's vineyard consulting business.

The idea for Hickory Creek and a partnership was planted after years of the friends interacting in the vineyard business. Mike helped Gottfried and David manage their vineyards and sell grapes to some of the larger area wineries. After three years of making wine in Mike's basement where, Mike laughs, "We bought way more grapes than we could make into wine and drink ourselves," they decided to put a business plan together to share their favorite wines.

Gottfried adds, "It's my mission to bring the styles of dry wines from where I'm from in the region of Franconia in Germany to our customers." Gottfried relocated to the United States after meeting his wife, Anne, at the university in Hamburg. Anne's family operates a bed-and-breakfast next to Gottfried's grapevines, while Gottfried and Anne live in Chicago full-time. Gottfried commutes to the winery when needed, especially during busier weekends.

Mike is also helping a friend, Javier Cardeñas, grow vines in Mexico along the high plains between mountain regions. Javi, who is a chef in New Buffalo, features his homemade hot sauce at the winery. You'll find other local products, like maple syrup, and featured artists from the region. "A lot of our friends are artists; we're excited to give them a place to showcase their art," Mike enthuses.

Gottfried adds, "We want to connect you to the art and process of winemaking. We are winemakers who are growers. We're farmers. Personally, I like to be connected to nature and watching the vineyard plants grow up."

Gottfried is also passionate about their wines, sharing that he loves the rosé, "It's smoky and powerful like those made in southern France and Spain." The Chardonnay he describes as "complex and crisp. It's a beautiful wine for white meat, seafood, and shellfish. It's a French style."

He believes, "Michigan has a huge potential for Rieslings and Pinot Noirs—two wines we're excited about. We know good wine. We opened a winery to share our love for wine and the style we love."

GET IN TOUCH

750 Browntown Road
Buchanan
(269) 422-1100
info@hickorycreekwinery.com
www.hickorycreekwinery.com
GPS: N 41° 54.07938, W 086° 28.34238

Karma Vista Vineyards

Six generations of Hermans have grown fruit amid southwest Michigan's gently rolling, fertile countryside. Joe and Sue Herman who, in 1990, began growing grapes for Welch's Grape Juice, represent the latest in 150 years of fruit farmers. "We were growing Concord and Niagara grapes for juice, and we thought, 'why not grow wine grapes?'" Joe reminisces.

Joe and Sue manage 500 acres of vineyards and orchards, growing wine and jelly grapes, cherries, and peaches. They grow wine grapes for some of the larger wineries in the region, including St. Julian. "I love it because it allows us to grow grapes on a bigger scale, rather than juggle a bunch of small blocks of vines," shares Joe. "We harvest the grapes we need for our wines and sell the rest."

Their newer passion for winemaking and cheerful perspectives are evident when Joe imparts that, as a rule, most new wineries are started by millionaires who don't know anything about grape growing but figure, "How hard can it be to learn?" While Joe and Sue, on the other hand, are grape growers who know nothing about being millionaires but figure, "Hey, how hard can it be to learn?"

We visited Joe and Sue's comfortably open tasting room and witnessed the charming couple's humor firsthand. We also soaked in the incredible view offered by Karma Vista's massive windows offering 360-degree views of grape vines and peach, apple, and cherry orchards.

During our visit, we learned that cherries are freshly picked from the family farm to make Cherri Amour, which Joe touts as tasting like "Mom's cherry pie in a bottle." Raspberry dessert wine Razz M'Tazz earned "Best of Class" at the Michigan Wine and Spirits Competition, after which proud winemaker Joe stated, "I seriously considered mounting the trophy as a hood ornament on my Jeep."

Shop elegant and funky wine and home accessories as you sample wines with monikers influenced by Pink Floyd, John Lennon, and the lost art of album covers: Pink Side of the Moon, a blend of Foch, Vidal, and Seyval; and Starry, Starry White, a semi-sweet blend with Riesling grapes.

Challenge your knack for music lyrics by reading the back of Stone Temple Pinot Noir; Joe and Sue often weave favorite verses into their wine descriptions. Other wines reflect the region, such as dry, red Côte d'Lôma (Hills of Coloma) and, more recently, movie humor.

If you're an Austin Powers fan, you'll love Joe's white Merlot label on his Mojo Noveau wine. "Remember, when you've got your mojo, you've got it all. Yeah baby!"

When we asked about the difference between a white Merlot and a typical Merlot, Joe explained, "A white Merlot is a much lighter shade of red. You leave the grapes soaking in their skins for only one day, rather than up to 10 days, as you do with Merlots you may be used to drinking." It results in a less heavy, or full-tasting, wine, pleasing to semidry red drinkers.

The Hermans' first vintage of Sauvignon Blanc was "accidental" when a batch of 150 grapevines mixed in with a Merlot planting. "We were so surprised to find the white grapes growing so well," Joe laughs. "We didn't think Sauvignon Blanc could grow in these soils, but it proved hardy enough." They made Sauvignon Blanc, which produced a "spectacular, white citrusy flavor." Joe plans additional vintages of the wine, as it was a huge hit with his customers.

Situated six miles as the crow flies from Lake Michigan and its temperate climate, Karma Vista relies heavily on this natural phenomenon for their multi-fruit harvest. As their long history of family farming can attest, the Hermans are passionate about risk taking. As Joe likes to share, "It's been a labor of love—and panic."

GET IN TOUCH

6991 Ryno Road
Coloma
(269) 468-9463
info@karmavista.com
www.karmavista.com
GPS: N42°10.74096, W086°17.36586

Lemon Creek Winery

In the far southwest corner of the Michigan "mitt" is Berrien County, home to the state's biggest fruit production region. Eight generations of the Lemon family have grown fruit here, earning the notable Michigan Sesquicentennial recognition for 150 years of farming.

More than half of the 300-acre farm is covered in traversing vines, making the farm also one of the biggest for grape growing. This significant footprint in Michigan's fruit history was initiated by Benjamin Lemon in 1855. Embracing the family's farming tradition and running the farm today are seventh-generation Lemons, Jeff, Tim, and Bob. Mom Helen is proprietor of the farm that sits on Lemon Creek Road and runs parallel to the small creek named in honor of the Lemon family. Helen and her husband, the late Robert Lemon, opened the winery in 1984.

Wines are 100 percent estate grown, benefiting from the moderating effect of Lake Michigan and rolling clay loam hills. Winemaker Jeff distinguishes Lemon Creek with one of his successes, Moon Shadow Cabernet Sauvignon Ice Wine. "We're the first in Michigan to make a red ice wine," he says.

Jeff also believes they are the only one in the United States to produce an ice wine from the Cabernet Sauvignon grapes, as most ice wines are produced with white grapes. Ice wines are made with frozen grapes handpicked off the vines and squeezed to get droplets of juice for making this specialty dessert-style wine. Another fun wine to look for is the Snow Shadow Vidal Blanc that is harvested during a full moon lunar eclipse.

flavor is received so well. "There are tons of people who keep coming back because they love the barbeque sauce," says Kaitlyn, eighth-generation Lemon and daughter to winemaker Jeff.

Another family member you'll run into is Tyson, part of the eighth generation of Lemons and son to Tim. Tyson assists with winemaking and other farming duties as needed. Rounding out the family members visible on the Sesquicentennial farm are Shadow, a formidable yet friendly canine and super-kind Annie, the family's golden retriever.

Make a day of your visit, tasting wines and picking fresh fruit from the orchards, loaded seasonally with raspberries, cherries, apples, peaches, plums, and nectarines. Pair your gathered fruit with Lemon Creek's Lighthouse White, made with 100 percent Seyval grapes, for a perfect afternoon accompaniment. Toast the Lemon family and their long-standing agricultural enterprise with fruity, smooth Sesquicentennial White.

The Lemons also grow Chardonnay, Pinot Grigio, Gewürztraminer, Shiraz, Cabernet Franc, and Merlot. Amid the grapevines and cherry trees, the tasting room is extended from a nineteenth-century barn and built with old wooden beams from the 1800s. The barn's large doors open wide on seasonally warm days, inviting cool breezes into the tasting room.

Sip wines crafted from grapes flourishing in centuries-old farmland and shop gourmet, locally produced goodies, such as jam, honey, and cheese. Stock up on Bob's "Uncle Bob's Homemade Barbeque Sauce," made with wine, of course, for summer grilling and adding sweet flavor to chicken, meatballs, and pork. The yummy sauce is a favorite of ours. We're frequently sending a bottle home with guests after a homemade barbeque dinner, as the

GET IN TOUCH

533 East Lemon Creek Road
Berrien Springs
(269) 471-1321
info@lemoncreekwinery.com
www.lemoncreekwinery.com
GPS: N 41° 57.45552, W 086° 26.75982

Peterson and Sons Winery

Wine without the headache or hangover? That is what Duane Peterson of Peterson and Sons Winery claims of their all-natural wines with no sulfites added. One of the very few wineries in the world that makes wine without chemicals or preservatives, Duane believes his natural wines avoid typical allergic reactions such as headaches.

Duane's winemaking began as a hobby. He made his first five gallons of rhubarb wine in his basement in 1982 after being inspired by homemade rhubarb wine he enjoyed at a dinner party. His experimental winemaking expanded that same year into cherry, red raspberry, Concord, and Delaware.

The following year, Duane lost his job as an insurance adjuster. "At first, I drank a lot of beer and did a lot of fishing with my friend, Norm, while I was contemplating my future," says Duane. Norm suggested that he go into the winemaking business, as friends and family really liked his wine. This seemed like a far-fetched idea, but it eventually inspired Duane to open Peterson and Sons Winery in the basement of his home in 1983.

Duane's first major crush was a family affair as his dad, two sons, and nephew helped him pick the grapes and crush them into juice to produce his first 25 barrels of wine. Today, he continues to produce all-natural fruit wines made with mostly Michigan fruit grown by local farmers. Duane, who considers himself a winemaker, not a farmer, states, "I don't grow anything but old and tired."

A to-the-point kind of guy, Duane believes that wine tasting is more straightforward than most people seem to think. "What you like to drink is all you need to know," he claims. He also shares his basic principle of tasting and buying. "You like or you don't like, you buy or you don't buy," states Duane, "but buy at least one bottle of wine or leave $2 for tasting."

Duane offers a wide selection of fruit wines including apricot, blueberry, and rhubarb-raspberry, as well as reds made with Concord and whites made with Seyval Blanc. Make sure you try his Cranberry wine—his most popular. As claimed on their Web site, "If you haven't tried wine made without the use of chemicals, you haven't tried wine with true fruit taste and aroma."

A very spiritual guy, Duane believes in angels and claims that everything he knows about winemaking has come to him in his dreams. He shares that a 1996 dream changed his overall process, dramatically improving the quality of his wines. What is the new process? He will never tell. Duane also believes in reincarnation and is certain he was a winemaker in two previous lives, once in Germany in the 1500s and once in Italy as a monk in the 1300s.

As the business continued to grow, Duane moved his winemaking process from the basement into the garage in 1984, and into the current 40-by-84-foot winery in 1988. However, you can still sample the wines in the original tasting room in the basement where Duane makes your tasting experience simple and easy.

GET IN TOUCH:

9375 East P Avenue
Kalamazoo
(269) 626-9755
www.naturalwine.net
GPS: N 42° 13.07286, W 085° 26.63166

Round Barn Winery

Thanks to the changing of Michigan laws to enable wineries to distill and sell brandies, a reconstructed, historic round barn sits amid Berrien County's rolling farmland. Vintner Rick Moersch is always quick to answer the frequent "Why a round barn?" "You won't find any bad spirits lingering here. The devil can't hide, if there aren't any corners," he smiles.

The round barn is the center of Rick's thriving operation that has grown to encompass a winery, distillery, and brewery. The round barn's doorway was handcrafted from pre–World War I redwood that Rick salvaged from one of Al Capone's infamous breweries. When we asked how he came into the wood, Rick laughingly replied, "That's another story I can't tell."

With the help of his dad, Rick used the wood to create several other accents on his property. These include a stunning, semicircular bar in the round barn, as well as the doors leading into a locked cellar holding 1,500 gallons of brandy below the 1881 post-and-beam barn where Round Barn's wines, microbrews, brandies, and vodka are available for tasting and sales.

Up to 250 tons of fruit are processed during harvest by Rick, with the help of wife Sherrie, sons Chris and Matt, and a small staff of skilled workers. "Harvest is my favorite time of year; I love R&D and formulating new wines," shares the former high school biology teacher.

the Internet and began researching round barns for my distillery." Rick found his round barn, abandoned and dilapidated in Indiana and two weeks from being burnt to the ground.

"Somehow I convinced Sherrie and the banker that I was dead serious about relocating this barn," tells Rick. He saved the 1911 round barn from demolition and hired Amish craftsmen to dismantle it, and then rebuild the barn on his farm in Baroda. Today, the round barn is the centerpiece of his property and widely used for weddings and other celebrations.

"I love coming through the doors with a glass of wine in hand and gazing up at the beamed ceiling—it's awe-inspiring," son Chris shares. As General Manager, Chris runs the winery's operations, as well as those of his new Free Run Cellars venture down the road with brother Matt. Matt has earned the reins of winemaker, distiller, and brewer at Round Barn and is winemaker at Free Run. The close-knit Moersch family applies biology skills and passion for "enjoying the ride" to give customers one of Michigan's most diverse experiences.

Rick finessed his skills as a winemaker at Tabor Hill for several years after getting called to help out with a fermenting issue. He planted his own vineyard in 1981, opening the winery as Heart of the Vineyard in 1992. The name was changed later to Round Barn Winery after it was most often referred to as "the winery with the round barn."

Rick gives St. Julian full credit for spearheading a "green project," in conjunction with Michigan State University in the 1990s, to support wineries and their interest in distilling and selling fruit brandies. "I was in Europe at the time the law went into effect," reminisces Rick. "I immediately jumped on

"We like to make wine from everything around here," observes Rick. He uses walnuts from his property for the winery's Walnut Liquor. The black walnuts are also blended in mouth-watering dishes, such as the Grilled Sirloin Burger seared in Black Walnut Pi Butter. Talented, self-taught cook Sherrie dreams up delicious recipes, which are prepared seasonally by the winery's chef and served in the Wine Cellar Café—"our outdoor grill," Rick describes—from Memorial Day through fall colors.

"We like to make wine from everything around here…"

Hand cut grapes to make your own wine.

After discovering delicious Mirabelle plums, popular in France and Austria, Rick found a West Coast source for the plums and planted nearly an acre. He's looking forward to crafting a flavorful plum brandy. In the meantime, enjoy customer favorites Black Currant Pi and Blackberry Pi; fruit was hand-picked from local farms to craft the cordials.

Under the round barn's pinnacle roof, Rick and his sons approach distilling and brewing as artisans, crafting small batches of cordials, brandies, micro-brews, and Michigan's first "vodka from the vineyard." Fresh fruit from the region is used to create the sweeter cordials and pure fruit brandies that have no added chemicals or artificial flavors. Handpicked grapes are distilled in a copper pot to create DiVine Vodka, the Midwest's first premium estate vodka.

You'll also find a diverse selection of wines, all made from fruits from the Moersch farm and the region. During one of our visits, Rick insisted we try his Apricot Demi-Sec. "It's like biting into a fresh apricot." Although we tried to bow out, fearing the wine might be too sweet for our drier palates, Rick convinced us to taste. Both of us took bottles home after discovering the wine did, indeed, appeal to our shared passion for not-too-sweet summertime, outdoor wines.

If you're a fan of Chianti, take home Vineyard Red, a blend of Chancellor and Chambourcin with a touch of oak. Red wine drinkers will also like the Moersch's Pinot Noir, Cabernet Sauvignon, and Merlot. And if you favor sweeter wines, taste best-selling Cranberry. "It's the only civilized way to have your cranberries," Rick firmly believes.

This family-run winery's entrepreneurial approach to winemaking and expanding their offerings is inspiring. When asked how ideas are generated, Rick shared, "I do a lot of reading of old English text. You know … we're not the first to do this." He also gives credit to his expert team of workers, including sons Chris and Matt, who have been with him for the long haul. "I couldn't do all this alone." He claims retirement is not too far off in the future, although we're sure this former biology teacher will always be experimenting with fruit.

As the only winery that offers hands-on winemaking classes that start in the vineyard cutting grapes in the fall and conclude with bottling wine in the spring, Round Barn's white and red wine classes fill up quickly. This isn't a class where you simply blend juices. You climb into the Moersch's hay-baled wagon and ride into one of their vineyards. There

Michigan's first vodka from the vineyard.

and hanging from the beams, remnants of the farm's working past. From a tap, Chris poured our chosen, handcrafted microbrews into one-gallon growlers to take home. We're looking forward to grabbing another growler on our next visit as the tasty amber brew didn't last long.

Round Barn Winery is a destination where we're sure you'll find a wine, or other beverage, to love. "All wines are local wines somewhere. Taste with an open mind," Rick encourages. "We honor the cranberry wine drinkers as well as the Pinot Noir drinkers. There are no shoulds or shouldn'ts here. Come celebrate with us."

you spend the morning cutting grapes off vines and filling up crates. Back in the winery, you dump grapes through the crusher and choose whether to store your wine in oak or glass over the winter.

Come spring, after determining the wine's desired sweetness level, you wash and fill bottles, and then cork and label two cases of wine. Rick advises cellaring the wine to best enjoy your full-flavored, self-made wine. The class is two days of fun, hanging with the Moersch family, and making wine in a truly relaxed atmosphere.

If you prefer having your drinks served to you, ready to go, spend time in the historic tasting room. Admire the rusted, well-worn tools decorating walls

GET IN TOUCH

10983 Hills Road
Baroda
(800) 716-9463
info@roundbarnwinery.com
www.roundbarnwinery.com
GPS: N 41° 55.20348, W 086° 27.49674

Tasting Room:
Union Pier
9185 Union Pier Road
(269) 469-6885
GPS: N 41° 49.68822, W 086° 40.683

St. Julian Winery

St. Julian bubbles with the activity of visitors who stream in and line up at the bar to taste wines from Michigan's oldest continuously run winery. More than 40 different wines and 10 juices are available to please everyone—from the first-time taster to the wine connoisseur. Behind this bustling, almost century-old operation, though, is a quiet underlying foundation: the upholding of winemaking traditions and the unwavering connection to family.

Proprietor and third-generation vintner Dave Braganini insights, "I try to perpetuate traditions established by my father and grandpa." Dave's grandfather, Mariano Meconi, founded Border City Wine Cellars in Windsor in 1921 after migrating from Faleria, Italy, at age 26. Following the repeal of prohibition in 1933, Mariano moved his winery across the river to Detroit and then to Paw Paw in 1936 to be closer to the Lake Michigan shore. St. Julian is the winery's fourth name, last changed from Italian Wine Company to avoid anti-Fascism during World War II and to honor the patron saint of Faleria, San Giuliano (St. Julian).

"My grandpa was an entrepreneur," Dave promptly replies when we ask him to describe his beloved grandfather. "Although he didn't want to grow. After advertising on Johnny Carson's *Tonight Show* he almost immediately stopped advertising. When I asked him why he stopped, he replied that he was selling too much wine. I believe you've got to keep going, or you'll dry up."

Perhaps his father, the late Apollo Braganini, ignited Dave's love of wine and the winemaking business.

"There just aren't enough grapes grown here," he expresses. "We're working to change that. We're growing Syrah and Sauvignon Blanc now. Pinot Grigio grows very well here, maybe better than anywhere else in the United States. It takes a good 30 to 40 years before you know what works. Grapes grow really, really well right here. Lake Michigan is blessed with the ability to grow grapes."

The winery started with Concord, Niagara, and Delaware grapes in the late 1930s, before planting French hybrids such as Seyval Blanc, Vignoles, and Maréchal Foch in the 1960s. More recently, St. Julian's winemaking team is crafting wines using more traditional European vinifera grapes under the Braganini Reserve label, including Pinot Noir, Riesling, and the Sauvignon Blanc. We've been enjoying their Chancellor for several years. And the Riesling has won an impressive string of gold medals, including "Best White Vinifera Wine in the East" at the Best of the East competition and gold at the San Francisco International Wine Competition, both in 2006.

"We picked grapes. I always liked it," Dave says. "You smell the grapes, you see the truck leave. I really like the fruit. With the grapes, every year you get another chance to do it again and hopefully do it better."

Today, grapes are planted by 100 growers in a 45-mile radius of Paw Paw. St. Julian also recently started a vineyard consulting business to oversee others' vineyards with the intent to buy grapes from the vines for use in future vintages.

The most successful wine of St. Julian's history in recent years is Blue Heron, a semisweet white wine blend of Riesling, Seyval Blanc, and Vignoles. Dave touts it was Michigan's top-selling wine for years and it wins a ton of awards. "It won gold at the Los Angeles County Fair," Dave shares during our visit one fall. He credits his late father, Apollo, for the wine's success.

"My dad lived on a lake. After he died, I'd go there and stand on the dock with a drink to reminisce.

Every time, a blue heron would fly by," Dave fondly recalls. "I believe my dad was telling me to make the Blue Heron wine. When we came out with it in 2000, it immediately became our top-selling wine." A half-million bottles are sold each year and it's the winery's most prevalent brand. "The Blue Heron recalls the good times."

Piggybacking on the wine's success, St. Julian released Red Heron in 2006, a semisweet red wine made with a secret blend that Dave says they won't reveal. It's their only wine blend that's a well-kept secret. What wasn't a secret during our visit was the testing of a new Sparkling Red Heron. Dave admits to testing a lot of different grapes and blends over the history of the winery.

It's evident by the number of people visiting St. Julian and the rotating tours that visitors are passionate for St. Julian and for getting a close look at what goes on behind the scenes. We, too, enjoyed a tour led by assistant winemaker Nancie Corum. Our first stop was to visit the laboratory where chief winemaker Dave Miller, PhD, and Nancie share work space.

Dr. Dave, as he is called, has applied his impressive research credentials in a real world environment at St. Julian. He worked as research manager in the Viticulture and Enology program at Michigan State University where he directed the vine physiology and enology lab for 13 years. Dr. Dave overhauled St. Julian's test laboratory when he first joined the winery in 1997 and now manages the grape grower relations, in addition to his daily winemaking duties.

Nancie shared with us that she joined St. Julian in 2002 and has been "creating her position" along the way, helping to extend the functions of the laboratory, applying expertise learned at Purdue University. The impressive wine testing laboratory, which may be Michigan's largest, is full of beakers and test tubes, reminding us of chemistry classes many moons ago.

After touring the lab, Nancie took us to the Olde Age Barrel Room, which is accessed down a sloping cement floor along antique grape and apple presses, which we later learned from Dave are one of his collector items—200 and counting. "The antigun lobbyist likes to get the guns out of the hands of the citizens; I like to get the wine presses out of the hands of the citizens," laughs Dave. "My father used to drive everyone crazy with them everywhere; to me, it's another link to the past."

60,000 cases per year. This is all the more impressive when you know that some of Michigan's smallest wineries produce fewer than 1,000 cases per year. During our tour, we watched the forest green bottles used for St. Julian's non-alcoholic Sparkling Wild Berry Spumante being gently plopped from their boxes onto the conveyor system before they moved single file through the system. The sparkling juice was automatically poured into each bottle; the bottles were topped with champagne-like toppers, foil, and labels; and then manually placed back in boxes. It takes five minutes for each bottle to go from start to finish on the conveyor system.

Northeast of Paw Paw is St. Julian's small Frankenmuth winery, notable for holding 1,000 barrels, many of which store the winery's most award-winning wine, Solera Cream Sherry, before bottling. The winery's records show that Solera Cream Sherry won 62 golds, some of which were double gold honors, through 2005. Sip the creamy sherry as an aperitif and indulge in the Solera Double Gold Truffle on the side, handcrafted by The Chocolate Garden of Coloma.

Watching the whirlwind of activity and learning about St. Julian's far-reaching impact on Michigan's wine industry, it's easy to forget that this winery's roots and day-to-day busy operations are entrenched in maintaining St. Julian's reputation and upholding the Braganini-Meconi family traditions.

"Wine is an art. It helps you get up and get motivated. It's creative," Dave firmly believes. "A taste is worth a thousand words."

Inside the barrel room, we were awed by 600 oak barrels stacked along walls and the reverent blessing of the wine by chanting monks, a continuously played loop that has been running for several years. Notably, a pilot program initiated by Dr. Dave applies the use of Michigan oak to add natural spice to wines. St. Julian is the first in the nation to use this homegrown oak; although they also use the American, French, and Hungarian oaks as well.

If you've toured smaller wineries, you'll quickly appreciate St. Julian's size. Ranked among the top 40 largest wineries in the nation, its size is most evident with the visual moving display of the number of cases filling up in the bottling area. Nearly 2,000 bottles a day seemingly dance their way through St. Julian's automated bottling system to produce nearly

"Wine is an art. It helps you get up and get motivated. It's creative."

GET IN TOUCH

716 South Kalamazoo Street
Paw Paw
(800) 732-6002
orders@stjulian.com
www.stjulian.com
GPS: N 42° 12.79338, W 085° 53.49504

Tasting Rooms:

Dundee
119 Waterstradt Commerce Drive
(734) 529-3700
GPS: N 41° 57.43812, W 083° 40.45836

Frankenmuth
127 South Main Street
(989) 652-3281
GPS: N 43° 20.12412, W 083° 44.2806

Union Pier
9145 Union Pier Road
(269) 469-3150
GPS: N 41° 49.68822, W 086° 40.6743

Parma
2110 North Concord Road
(517) 531-3786
GPS: N 42° 15.45774, W 084° 36.0036

Michigan Oak: The New Spice

St. Julian's assistant winemaker Nancie Corum describes why different types of oak barrels, like French and Hungarian, are used: "Oak is like a spice rack; it adds different flavors. Each type of grain adds different amounts of caramel and vanilla, although the spices are generally the same within the region from which the barrels are grown."

The use of Michigan oak to age wines has been initiated by St. Julian through a pilot program. Oak logs from a forest in Van Buren County are sent to Kentucky, cut into staves, and then shipped back to St. Julian to age for two to three years in Michigan's climate. They are then sent back to Kentucky to a cooper for barrel production before returning to St. Julian to age select wines. Vintner Dave Braganini shares that, "It's so cold here; Michigan oak pores are smaller than regular oak. The spice is very subtle. It has incredible finesse."

Look for wines aged in Michigan oak at wineries throughout the state, as St. Julian has provided the barrels to every winery. "If we're all using Michigan oak, it becomes a great story for Michigan. No one else in the country is doing it," says Dave.

A Banquet of Collectibles

Antique lovers and vintage motorcycle fans must be sure to visit St. Julian and request a tour of the Apollo banquet hall. Better yet, sign up to attend a winemaker's dinner where you'll be surrounded by eclectic collectibles through your wine and dining experience. Some of the unique collectibles include:

• 1958 Panhead Harley Davidson motorcycle
• 1968 650 Firebird BSA
• Beatles and Elvis collectibles
• 1948 Harley Davidson police bike
• 1970 Triumph Bonneville
• Transistor radios

Motorcycles and grape presses hang overhead while a stunning oval oak table made from old oak barrel staves stands firmly on the ground. The collectibles are a lasting tribute to the family's history and, in particular, to Apollo Braganini and Mariano Meconi, founder of St. Julian.

Tabor Hill Winery & Restaurant

An elegant and fun celebration of great wine and great food awaits you at Tabor Hill, one of the state's oldest wineries. The celebration is yours to make; Tabor Hill provides the backdrop with its lovely vineyard country setting and warm welcome sign, "Drink wine, laugh often, live long." We propose adding "eat well" to their classic sign as Tabor Hill's chef creates artfully prepared, fresh, seasonal food that is superb and richly fulfilling.

The lodge-style restaurant opened 15 years after the planting of French hybrid grapevines established Tabor Hill in 1968, with the first wines released in 1972. General Manager Paul Landeck believes they have the oldest French hybrid vineyard in the state— and possibly even in the nation.

"We're most proud of the fact that we raise our own grapes, and produce and bottle our wine; everything is turnkey," enthuses Paul. "A new production winery was built within the last four years and 10,000 square feet of space were added to our tasting room and restaurant."

Owned by Dave and Linda Upton since 1976, Tabor Hill is truly a celebration of the marriage of food and wine, with wine itself being a food to be savored. Dave, whose father founded Whirlpool, has always had a fondness for wine. Together with Linda, who is publisher of Chicago-based *Dining* magazine, Dave invested in Tabor Hill in the early years before opting to become proprietor of the winery.

Another member of the team is winemaker Mike Merchant, who has been with the winery for more than 25 years. The winery's most popular wine, and one of its first to be produced, is the Classic Demi-Sec, a proprietary blend of five grapes. Bob Hope was a longtime fan of the dryer white wine and, after President Gerald Ford served the wine during his tenure at the White House, it continued to be served to U.S. Presidents for years.

"It outsells all our other wines and has won the most awards of any wine in the Midwest," shares Paul, who is genuinely hospitable, enjoying his work behind the scenes to ensure your Tabor Hill experience is memorable.

The winery's Red Arrow Red, named for nearby Red Arrow Highway, is another customer favorite that Tabor Hill's chef pairs with heartier, fall fare, including his rack of lamb and premium filet mignon, when featured on the menu. Every day, you'll find a mouth-watering menu with Tabor Hill classics, such as the raspberry chicken and grape-leaf-wrapped Norwegian salmon, as well as fresh fare updated daily and designed to complement wine cellar selections.

"Our chef works closely with Mike to create meals that complement vintages," explains Paul. To ensure the production of high-quality wines, Mike oversees the harvesting of grapes by hand from the winery's 40 acres of grapes and from more than 300 acres of vines under contract with area growers. All vines are within the Lake Michigan Shore AVA, a designated wine-growing region in Michigan's southwest corner.

Dave offers a celebration of great food and great wine.

Mike has had a significant impact on Tabor Hill's evolving wine production and the pairing of wine with food, believing "We're known for our German-style wines, which lend themselves well to being paired with a number of dishes." Mike joined Tabor Hill in 1979 as vineyard manager, after earning a degree in horticulture from Michigan State University. "I learned quickly that the winemaker calls all the shots in the vineyard." Mike earned the position and never looked back. When we asked Mike what keeps him passionate for winemaking, he quickly replied, "The vineyard. By producing the highest quality fruit I can, making the wine is like

Rosé. A 2003 Merlot and 2005 Pinot Noir were also paired with the lovely appetizer presentation of smoked Gouda, duck confit empanada, grilled shrimp skewers, butter-roasted apples, and fresh strawberries. The food was lively and fresh, and matched perfectly with Tabor Hill's wine selection to bring out the fare's subtle hints of flavors.

"Reservations are recommended on summer weekends and when fall colors are peaking," Paul advised. "Although, please drop in any time. In many cases, we can seat you and, of course, we always want to seat you."

You're invited to partake in a vineyard and cellar tour, which may be led by the very personable Kenny Petersen who oversees wine sales and assists with ensuring a remarkable experience. Kenny is thrilled to be learning the winemaking trade under Mike's direction in his very spare time.

"I grew up in the area, running around this property with the Moersch brothers when their dad was winemaker here," laughs Kenny. "A lot of people I've known have taught me great things. It has been a yellow-brick-road kind of experience." His attention to detail was learned from "Uncle Paul" who excels in hospitality.

The Tabor Hill team is friendly and personable and very willing to share tips about enjoying the wine. Other wines to taste at the large bar are the dry Riesling, which Mike describes as their showpiece, "We're very proud of it." Paul also encourages you to try the Kerner, "It's really hot."

falling off a log. It's easy as long as you have good fruit from the vines. When Mother Nature gives us challenging growing circumstances, I finesse the canopies and manipulate crop loads as needed to get the fruit to be what it needs to be."

Growing in Tabor Hill's vineyard are many varietals, including Riesling, Chardonnay, Pinot Noir, and Baco and Chancellor Noirs. Newer to the land is Syrah, Lemberger, and Merlot, evidence of Mike's interest in expanding their red wine offerings. "The workhorse of red wines, though, is Cabernet Franc. Its hardiness makes it grow very well here. It produces astounding fruit that we use for different products, including a rosé and port."

Ecstatic to dine at the restaurant after two attempts to get in without reservations during busy harvest time, our tasting experience included a flight of red wines, including the yummy 2005 Cabernet Franc

He says the Riesling hybrid has very distinct flavors like "citrus, apple, peach, and apricot" ...

Mike describes the Kerner as "a cornucopia of flavors." He says the Riesling hybrid has very distinct flavors like "citrus, apple, peach, and apricot" that you can taste individually. Another limited-edition, distinctive wine is Tabor Hill's ice wine, made with Vidal Blanc grapes picked frozen from the vine at about 17- to 20-degree temperatures. "The juice is like nectar. Its flavor is magical." The ice wine has around 13% residual sugar and is 12 percent alcohol.

Tabor Hill is a destination where you can easily spend the afternoon tasting, dining, and touring the vineyard and winery. Head to the Grape Escape Lounge or lodge-style dining area lined with large glass windows, giving you the feeling of sitting in the vineyard, which, in essence, you are. The warm, inviting interior is accented with a gaslit fire in the fieldstone fireplace and, most notably, by the fresh flower arrangements on each table and beautifully positioned throughout the winery.

"We feel these simple, yet deliberate, touches create a classy environment," Paul expresses. "You can be comfortable here, and we'll make things as pretty as they can be," Paul adds, sweeping his arm toward the fresh flowers and vineyard view.

GET IN TOUCH

185 Mount Tabor Hill
Buchanan
(800) 283-3363
info@taborhill.com
www.taborhill.com
GPS: N 41° 54.84084, W 086° 27.34194

Tasting Rooms:
Benton Harbor Wine & Art Gallery
80 W Main Street
(269) 925-6402
GPS: N 42° 6.9411, W 086° 27.37212

Saugatuck Wine Port
214 Butler Street
(269) 857-4859
GPS: N 42° 39.35658, W 086° 12.25716

Bridgman Champagne Cellar
10243 Red Arrow Highway
(269) 465-6566
GPS: N 41° 55.53504, W 086° 34.44288

Warner Vineyards

A charming covered wooden bridge over the Paw Paw River takes you to another world, secreting you away just seconds off the main thoroughfare. The flowing river and small waterfall drown out any street noise, and your step immediately slows down to its soothing rhythm. Walk under the vine-covered trellis to Warner Vineyards, Michigan's second-oldest continuously run winery.

You'll often be greeted by one of the third-generation Warner brothers, James, Bill, or Patrick. A fourth brother, Tom, lives in Florida and while he isn't involved in the day-to-day operations, Pat shares that he certainly enjoys the wines. You may also get a friendly welcome from Vino, the family's 11-pound Chihuahua they humorously refer to as their security dog. "Everybody needs a little vino," chuckles Pat.

John Turner and James Warner, Pat's grandfather and father, respectively, founded the winery in 1938 under the name of Michigan Wineries, as an adjunct to the family's banking, farm supply, and farming businesses. The winery's history began during the Depression after they gained possession of land owned by grape growers. With vineyards in hand, an expected frost that year, and a very short window to make a decision, the two decided to start their own winery. The vineyards survived the frost and the winery continued to operate, changing its name a couple times until it became Warner Vineyards in 1973.

Today, Warner Vineyards continues to flourish, earning rave reviews for Warner Brut Sparkling Wine, honored with being served in the White House by President Gerald Ford in 1976 and selected as the

Notably, the Warners still use an antique disgorging unit.

official champagne of Super Bowls XXXIII in 1982 and XL in 2006. "It's our flagship," Pat proudly states.

Notably, the Warners still use an antique disgorging unit. When we asked about the unique-looking rustic equipment, Pat laughs, replying, "It's older than you and me. It's easily a hundred years old or more. We use it to hand bottle, label, and hand cork our Warner Brut."

Other Warner stars are the Cabernet Sauvignon, a limited-edition, dry, full-bodied red that has been rated among the best by *Wine Savant* magazine. Other flavorful reds include Cabernet Franc, Merlot, and, one of our favorites to stock in our cellars, Veritas. Veritas, meaning "truth" in Latin, is a big, soft balanced red. Solera Port Dessert Wine is their most award-winning wine, says Pat. The deep, ruby-colored aperitif is bold and sinfully delicious.

The smooth, silky white Liebestrauben, German for "Grapes of Love," is their number one seller, which they claim has "great legs and an excellent body." The ultra crisp Pinot Grigio is a must for sipping porch-side on a warm summer evening. Warner offers "bone dry to dessert wines" and everything in between; we're sure you'll find a wine to love. Indeed, Warner is the place to be in the summer with "Taste the Art and Jazz" on weekend evenings on their large outdoor patio along the picturesque Paw Paw River. "We have bands on the weekends, and people love to sit by the river and listen to a little jazz," shares Pat.

Architecture buffs will appreciate the 1898-built village waterworks structure that was renovated in 1967 with lumber from old wine casks. Kevin's Tavern on the River has since moved into the space; a white-tablecloth, elegant restaurant serving light appetizers to full entrees. A historic water tower juts through the skyline behind the winery, boasting the name Cask Wine, a former name of the winery.

Sure to catch your eye in the tasting room is the European-style Champagne cave that gives you a feeling that you're in the south of France. Venture into the neighboring 1914 Grand Trunk Railroad passenger rail car, relocated by the Warners for intimate private party gatherings. A stop at Warner's Vineyard is an opportunity to taste time-perfected wines and unwind next to "Ye Olde Wine Haus" along the river.

GET IN TOUCH:

706 South Kalamazoo Street
Paw Paw
(800) 756-5357
pat@warnerwines.com
www.warnerwines.com
GPS: N 42° 17.66622, W 085° 35.56344

Tasting Room:
South Haven
515 Williams Street
(269) 637-6900
GPS: N 42° 24.2955, W 086° 16.38702

Kevin's Tavern on the River

Escape into the quaint and cozy atmosphere of Kevin's Tavern on the River, located through the courtyard to Warner Vineyards, for delicious gourmet fare with local flavors. The elegant, white-tablecloth restaurant serves light appetizers to full entrees to desserts. From hamburgers to filet mignon, Kevin's offers food for whatever your mood.

Chef Kevin Hyman adds flavor with a variety of herbs grown fresh in his small garden on top of the hill behind the restaurant. You'll love his homemade lavender thyme butter spread on fresh mini loaves of Italian bread, which not only tastes good but provides a soft lavender aroma through the air. You also can't go wrong with the Pecan Chicken, as Kevin describes, "It's prepared with Warner's Peach and Honey wine, which I cook to reduce the alcohol and add cream and nutmeg for a wonderful flavor."

We look forward to dining at Kevin's any time of the year as his signature dishes are inspired by fresh local produce of the season. From strawberry chicken to cherry chicken to radishes and asparagus, you're sure to savor every bite (269) 657-5165.

Leelanau Peninsula Wine Trail 🖉

LEELANAU PENINSULA AVA

Known for its lake vistas *and pure beauty, Leelanau Peninsula is home to a growing number of wineries. Being "up north," Leelanau is a cool climate grape growing region, so variety and clone selection has been critical— to ensure both ripe flavors in the fruit and vine survival over the cold winters. The omnipresent Lake Michigan is the real key to our success. The "Big Lake" keeps us cool in the spring, delaying bud break and helping growers avoid spring frosts, and keeps us warm into the fall, prolonging the ripening season to help develop the wonderful flavors found in Leelanau Peninsula wines. The "lake effect" moderates winter temperatures, which allows us to grow the tender old-world vinifera varieties. Though many varieties are grown, there is consensus that the white varieties Riesling, Pinot Gris, and Chardonnay and the reds Pinot Noir and Cabernet Franc are quite well suited to Leelanau Peninsula.*

"World Class" has been bandied about for these varieties by customers and critics. An identifiable regional character that transcends winery style seems to be emerging for some of the aforementioned varieties. Grape growers tend to select south, southeast, and southwest facing slopes to capture additional warmth from the sun. The slopes help ensure good air drainage to move cold air off-site. Vineyard soils tend to range from loamy sand to sandy loam and even to clay on some sites, with old lake bed shale present in some soils. This leads to an interesting array of flavors that local winemakers have taken advantage of to create wines in a variety of styles, offering exquisite fruit-forward wines that are a in world class of their own.

—Charlie Edson, Ph D, Vintner
Bel Lago Winery

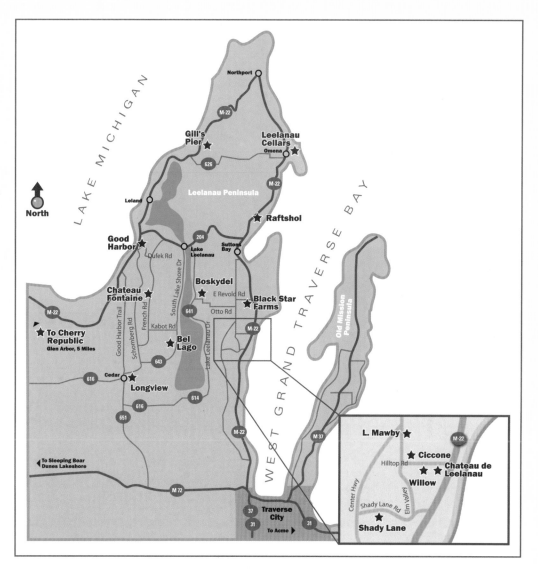

Bel Lago Vineyard and Winery

Bel Lago Vineyard and Winery is named for the "beautiful lake" that gives customers one of the region's unparalleled views of the sandy-bottom Lake Leelanau that extends 23 miles along Leelanau Peninsula.

Bel Lago's farm with nearly 30 acres of vines is a life's dream for winemaker Dr. Charlie Edson and his wife Dr. Amy Iezzoni. "Small towns and lakes are my thing," says the Whitehall native. "I can't imagine living anywhere else or doing anything else. I've always imagined being a farmer with a lake view."

Charlie attended the University of Michigan for a couple of years after high school before transferring to Michigan State University. "I switched to MSU for horticulture," shares Charlie, who continued his education at MSU to earn a bachelor's degree, a master's degree, and a Ph.D. in horticulture.

Charlie was working toward earning his master's degree when he met up with Dr. Stan Howell. "I was working on an apple project, and I met Dr. Howell and found out what he was doing and immediately started making wine." Charlie focused on experimental wines under the supervision of Dr. Howell and was the first to craft late-harvest Vignoles and Vignoles ice wine along with the help of another student, Dave Miller, Ph.D, now the winemaker at St. Julian Wine Company.

Charlie continues to produce ice wine, using Pinot Grigio grapes frozen on the vines. He describes the very sweet dessert-style wine as "exquisite with apricot, honey, peach, and pear flavors." Notably, his crisp, medium-bodied Pinot Grigio wine won double gold at the Michigan State Fair and gold at the Riverside California International Wine Competition.

Charlie and Amy, along with Amy's parents Domenic and Ruth Iezzoni, planted the farm's first vines in 1987 on a one-acre test plot. The planting was a momentous family occasion, as Domenic's father, the grandson of an Italian wine merchant, sold two barrels of wine as a young adult for passage to the United States. Today, Domenic, an active physician at the age of 82, still cherishes the key to his great-grandfather's old wine cellars in Italy, and the family embraces their Italian heritage, as is evident by the winery's moniker.

The family opened their tasting room just over 10 years after planting their first vines on an old fruit farm. You must visit Bel Lago to appreciate the vista views of Lake Leelanau and Charlie's unique wine blends. Although Charlie retired from MSU in 2001 to run the winery full-time, Amy continues her work as a horticulture professor at MSU.

"Our test plots allow us to see what grows best in our soil," says Charlie. He has proven that diverse grape varietals thrive in the sloping farmland. One of the few to grow Auxerrois in the region and the first to introduce it to the state, Charlie has also experimented with and expanded beyond the test plot to plant Pinot Grigio, Chardonnay, Cayuga White, Riesling, Gewürztraminer, and European classic varieties required for dry blends and sparkling wines, such as Pinot Noir, Merlot, and Regent.

Today, Charlie's advanced test site hosts over 80 different varietals. "Most are used in winemaking; many are used to provide breadth of flavor," says Charlie.

The friendly winemaker gave us a quick tour of his lakeside vineyard, pointing out the dandelions and milkweed intertwined with his vines' roots. "We don't clear away the weeds; they provide much-needed, natural nourishment to the vines, although a good balance is key," he gracefully teaches. The good-humored doctor was quick to jump atop the vines when we asked him for a photograph.

The very healthy-looking vines are amassed with grape varietals that have been blended by Charlie for past vintages into wines earning numerous medals through the years.

"Winemaking is an art, similar to gourmet cooking."

His premier dry red wine, Tempesta, is a deep, full-flavored Cabernet Franc blended with Merlot and aged in American oak. His Tempesta was rated a "world-class red" and Brut Sparkling wine as "one of Michigan's best" by Tom Stevenson, who is author of the impressive *The Sotheby's Wine Encyclopedia* book series.

"Winemaking is an art, similar to gourmet cooking," shares Charlie, who likes to create unique flavors through blending. "I like to use different varieties as spice."

"Our Chardonnay is a crowd pleaser," Charlie claims. We happen to agree; we timed our visit perfectly to taste Charlie's Chardonnay straight out of the barrel and compare it to another Chardonnay barrel tasting he was overseeing for a new winery. While the wines were deliciously distinct from one another, Charlie's resonated with lingering fruit notes. The winery's most popular white wine, Leelanau Primavera, is made with crisp, fresh aromas of apple, pear, and citrus—six different fruits altogether.

The Leelanau Conservancy is supported with a purchase of Conservancy Crystal River Cuvee. The delicious cuvee is a blend of Chardonnay, Auxerrois, Vignoles, and other select grape varieties with pear, peach, pineapple, and citrus notes. A percentage of sales goes to the conservancy, a nonprofit organization dedicated to protecting Lake Leelanau's watershed for continued enjoyment by anglers, boaters, and swimmers alike.

It's clear the winemaker doesn't take his beautiful scenery and lake view for granted. On early summer mornings, as you cruise between Cedar and the town of Lake Leelanau, you may just find Charlie kicking back on his small boat, afloat on the calm, azure lake where he's smiling up at his family's vineyard.

GET IN TOUCH

6530 South Lake Shore Drive
Cedar
(231) 228-4800
info@bellago.com
www.bellago.com
GPS: N 44° 53.04078, W 085° 43.47216

Black Star Farms

Hillside vines cascade alongside your drive into the estate of Black Star Farms while sleek-coated horses graze in open green pastures and equestrians practice dressage within the majestic red barn. Inn guests leisurely lounge on the sparkling white-columned veranda, while wine tasters stream into the nearby tasting room. This harmonious red-and-white colonial setting projects polite southern charm in its northern Michigan setting that lively awakens and bustles at harvest time.

Black Star Farms is a vision shared by proprietors Don Coe and grower Kerm Campbell. Together with winemaker Lee Lutes, the trio sought property with visual appeal where they could grow value-added agriculture and demonstrate farming as an active, viable business. They acquired the dormant horse farm with the existing mansion, stables, and riding arena and revitalized the property as an agricultural destination. A world-class equestrian facility, luxurious bed-and-breakfast inn, vineyard and winery, and award-winning creamery are part of the "wow-factor" you'll experience.

"Our vision is to connect wine with the land," states Don. "Wine is produced from a vine rooted in the vineyard—it doesn't just appear on supermarket shelves." The stunning tasting room invites you to linger with its roomy circular flow around the expansive bar while keeping you connected with the outdoors through the peaked glass windows overhead. Under the sky, sip wines and spirits as you watch renowned cheese-makers John and Anne Hoyt through large, glass windows.

The 2004 Pinot Noir also earned a gold medal at the 2006 Great Lakes Wine Competition, with Black Star Farms sweeping up a total of six golds at the competition. Other wines earning praise for the company they keep are the winery's 2002 A Capella Ice Wine, Sirius Maple Dessert Wine, and 2004 Arcturos Pinot Gris; all have had the honor of being served in the White House.

Lee, who attributes much of his wines' success to his vines, oversees winery operations, from vine management to bottling, hustling alongside his team of workers during October's harvest. One hundred and twenty acres of vines on Leelanau and Old Mission peninsulas are under Lee's attentive care.

"It's not rocket science. Man has been making wine for 1,000 years," enthuses Lee. "Good wine is made by attention to the details: management of vineyards and people; biology; and clean winemaking facilities."

On a vineyard walk with Bear, his black Labrador, Lee demonstrates the importance of balancing the vines with the fruit. He points out how the Maréchal Foch vines are planted six feet apart, while another varietal is planted four feet apart and the number of grape clusters differ as well. Lee inspects a healthy bunch of grapes, looking closely to determine its harvest readiness. "You want to look at the ripeness of seeds; are they turning brown? You also want to taste the grape for sugar levels and look for flavor. Each grape is different." Lee inspects grapes for color,

Many of the winery's 25 wines and brandies have earned medals from state, national, and international competitions. Arcturos Pinot Noir is among Black Star's shining stars, attracting the attention of world-renowned wine authority Tom Stevenson.

In Stevenson's fourth edition of *The Sotheby's Wine Encyclopedia*, which references classic wines of the world, he calls Black Star Farms "Michigan's superstar boutique winery." He further adds, "Lutes even manages to bring a touch of class to hybrids, making a yummy Red House Red from a blend of Maréchal Foch, Dornfelder, Regent, and Cabernet Franc." He rated the wines as "very exceptional; the local equivalent of a Bordeaux super second." Perhaps Stevenson's highest praise is when he refers to Lee as "this state's most gifted red-winemaker."

"I'm cyclonic," Lee enthuses. "In spring, I'm relaxed and enjoying life and its new vitality. In the fall and winter, I get busy. I love the lifestyle of a winemaker."

A few miles up the road from the farm, a truly unique pear orchard grows. Each spring when buds begin to spark on the trees, Lee directs his hardworking crew to place and tie wine bottles over each bud. Over the summer, Bartlett pears grow within the bottles, which are plucked off the trees in early September for production of their Pear and Its Spirit.

"Our pear brandy is part of our lore," informs Don. "It's evidence of our focus on agriculture. Rather than see houses built on this pear orchard, we worked with the grower to create a value-added product." The winery's pear brandy is one of its most talked about distilled spirits, because of its uniqueness. "One bottle of spirits is crafted by pure distillation of 15 to 20 pounds of fermented prime fruit."

texture, and taste before opting to harvest, a process that can take weeks or seemingly overnight when Mother Nature surprises us with a fall snowstorm.

This winemaker feels as one with nature and its dynamics, perhaps resulting from his early nomadic life living out of a 1964 station wagon with his parents in Australia for three years, starting at age seven. "It wasn't how we were doing it, rather it was the fact that we were doing it and living it," Lee fondly recalls. This early experience, followed by, in his later youth, growing up in northern Michigan, then living on the East Coast and overseas, led Lee to eventually return to the area to be as close to the land as possible.

For grappa fans, Black Star Farms crafts both a White Grape Grappa, made from the fresh must of Riesling, Gewürztraminer, and Vignoles, and a Red Grape Grappa, made from the fresh must of Pinot Noir, Cabernet Franc, and Merlot. Both grappas have won a handful of awards including double gold at the Taster's Guild International Wine Judging for the Red Grape Grappa. The smooth, aromatic finishes are 40 percent alcohol. Sipping grappa after dinner is an Italian tradition believed to assist the digestion of food.

The Arcturos brand is often seen on Black Star Farms' wine labels. Arcturos is derived from the Greek *Arktouros* and the Latin *Arcturus*, the giant star of the constellation Boötes, the guardian of the bear. The name was chosen in honor of the Sleeping Bear Dunes National Lakeshore.

Black Star Farms' hard apple cider also can't be beat, according to the *Wall Street Journal* in one of its 2006 weekend columns. It states the cider, "without trying to impersonate wine achieves that key characteristic of good vino—the long finish."

Stretch your experience with a getaway stay at the Inn at Black Star Farms. The exceptional beauty of the inn with its stone-wrapped fountain and white-covered portico is reflected inside with a dramatic staircase and white marble foyer accented with the Black Star Farms star.

Enjoy a spacious room with Jacuzzi, red-bricked fireplaces, and private veranda for shared intimacy over chilled sparkling wine. On your pillow each night, you'll find artisan-crafted truffles made by Grocer's Daughter Chocolate with Rainforest Alliance Certified chocolate that envelops the winery's Sirius Cherry Dessert Wine or Spirit of Cherry, a delicious fruit brandy.

Trails ideal for hiking, snowshoeing, and cross-country skiing surround the property and lead you to restful views of Grand Traverse Bay and Power Island, a nature preserve once owned by Henry Ford. Adjacent to the equestrian facility is a small petting zoo where young family members can get eye-to-eye with friendly farm animals.

Back in Lee's winemaking domain during early harvest time, Lee was inspired to share a "winemaker's mimosa"—straight Chardonnay juice from just-pressed grapes. Sipping the wonderfully surprising drink, thick with the consistency of honey, a can't-be-held-back satisfied sigh escapes. Lee charmingly smiles, "No worries."

GET IN TOUCH

10844 East Revold Road
Suttons Bay
(231) 271-4970
info@blackstarfarms.com
www.blackstarfarms.com
GPS: N 44° 56.14002, W 085° 38.05632

Tasting Room:
Old Mission Peninsula
360 McKinley Road East
Traverse City
Black Star Farms Old Mission
(231) 932-7416
GPS: N 44° 47.76978, W085° 34.14954

Leelanau Cheese Company

A true cheese lover won't be able to visit Black Star Farms without drooling at the window overlooking the cheese production at Leelanau Cheese Company, located within the tasting room. Proprietors and cheese makers John and Anne Hoyt offer homemade, cellar-aged, European-style cheese produced with milk from a local dairy farm.

Their signature cheese, very delicious Raclette, popular in both Switzerland and France, is offered in mild, sharp, and extra sharp forms—the same cheese aged at 3 months, 8 to 10 months, and 24 to 36 months consecutively. Ageing takes place in the cheese cave where the wheels of cheese are turned, washed, and brushed with salt water by hand every day to develop excellent flavor.

It didn't take long for us to start grabbing the small slabs of tasty cheese, and it disappeared quickly—we now stay stocked by buying the whole wheel. We even went the extra mile and bought the Girolle Originale Cheese Scraper that delicately shaves smooth pieces of Raclette into small flowerlike pieces— a great hit at dinner parties (231) 271-2600.

Grocer's Daughter Chocolate

Freshly picked herbs, edible flowers from the garden, and ripe fruit from orchards are blended with Rainforest Alliance Certified chocolate by Mimi Wheeler, whose mother was a grocer in rural Denmark where Mimi grew up. The resulting divine chocolate is making headlines for its all-natural artisan craftsmanship.

Lustrous truffles and puddles—mouthwatering pools of dark chocolate—are a few of the specialties Mimi whips up in her Empire retail shop and production facility. We discovered Grocer's Daughter Chocolate when we picked up a yummy truffle set delicately crafted with Black Star Farms' cherry dessert wine. Puddles and herb truffles were later savored during Leelanau Peninsula's annual Snowshoe Stomp and Taste the Passion weekend, making us devout followers of Mimi's all-natural chocolates.

Visit the Empire store along the Sleeping Bear Dunes National Lakeshore, or spot the chocolates at other retail outlets such as Zingerman's Deli in Ann Arbor. Located roughly 10 minutes south of Cherry Republic Winery in Glen Arbor and 20 minutes west of Longview Winery in Cedar, Grocer's Daughter Chocolate makes for a delicious side jaunt to Lake Michigan's protected shoreline.

GET IN TOUCH

12020 Leelanau Highway (M-22)
Empire
(231) 326-3030
GPS: N 44° 48.44562, W 086° 3.31506
thegrocersdaughter@gmail.com
www.grocersdaughter.com

Boskydel Vineyard

Grape-growing pioneer Bernie Rink took a gamble on Leelanau Peninsula's appellation more than 40 years ago, igniting northern Michigan's now-booming wine industry. He believed the peninsula's cool climate, sandy soil, and location along the forty-fifth parallel—a latitude shared with southern France and northern Italy wine regions—were ideal conditions for growing grapes. In 1964, Bernie planted French-American hybrid grapevines, a decision that played a vital role in Michigan's wine industry.

Bernie's decision to grow grapes was prompted by reading a book about winemaking while working in his 30-year career as a library director at Northwestern Michigan College. Bernie also knew that his five boys would stay out of trouble if they were too busy working in the fields. His dry sense of humor is evident when he talks of his boys and chuckles, "Every time I sat on the couch next to my wife, I got another son."

As Bernie's eldest son, Jim Rink, describes in an article titled "Field of Dreams in Leelanau County," in a reversal of the magical *Field of Dreams* scenario, Bernie replaced the boys' handmade baseball diamond with grapevines in 1964. The boys grew up learning the importance of a strong work ethic, not much different from Bernie's upbringing. His first exposure to growing grapes was as a young boy in Ohio. "I grew up on vineyards in the 1930s in Cleveland near Lake Erie," Bernie relates.

Bernie grows only French-American hybrid grapes, subscribing to the French "dying vine theory," which broadly states that the harder a vine has to struggle

to survive, the better the wine. He also believes that this allows him to produce higher quality wines at much lower prices.

Bernie opened his tasting room in 1976, naming Boskydel after a never-published manuscript by a friend who gave him "The Elves of Bosky Dingle" to read to his boys. Later, Bernie discovered that combining "Bosky," meaning shrubs or brush, and "dell" meaning a glen or valley, in old English, also means tipsy—sometimes appropriate in the winemaking business.

You can sample his 100-percent estate-grown wines in his eclectic pole barn tasting room cluttered with original artwork and favorite sayings collected over the years. It will most likely be Bernie himself who pours your samples at the small wine bar, only accommodating up to eight tasters— just the way Bernie likes it.

Bernie is affectionately referred to as "the wine Nazi" in northern Michigan, reminding people that the purpose in tasting the wines is to determine which ones you would like to purchase. "When people come in and drink a bottle, then purchase a bottle, I call that breaking even," says Bernie.

It's apparent that Bernie likes to keep things simple. "There's nothing for sale but wine," Bernie informs; and as his Web site states, "We offer zero percent financing—which means we don't take credit cards."

Bernie has played a visionary role in northern Michigan's winemaking history with his mission to "bring good quality wines to ordinary people at a reasonable cost." It's no wonder that Bernie has many repeat customers. It's easy to stock up on his wines; all are very affordably priced, including Vignoles, a dry spicy wine with a crisp aftertaste, and Bernie's favorite, De Chaunac, a dry red wine.

Your visit to Boskydel Vineyard in its natural countryside setting affords a landscape view of north Lake Leelanau, adding to the charm of meeting northern Michigan's first grape grower and legendary winemaker.

GET IN TOUCH

7501 East Otto Road
Lake Leelanau
(231) 256-7272
userg@jimrink.com
www.boskydel.com
GPS: N 44° 56.19786, W 085° 42.34602

Chateau de Leelanau Vineyard and Winery

You can take the girl out the farm, but you can't take the farm out of the girl. When cardiologist Dr. Roberta Kurtz needed an outlet from her busy practice serving heart patients, she bought an old 100-acre cherry and apple orchard in Leelanau Peninsula's hilly northern country to give her plenty of room to mow grass. "Mowing relaxes me," says the doctor, who grew up on a sheep farm in Ohio.

Roberta was prompted to make the purchase when her friend, the late Joanne Smart, encouraged her to buy the farm. "I said 'if it's such a good idea, why don't you put up some of your money as well,'" Roberta laughs.

The two friends purchased the farm in 1987 and, in 1989, replaced just over a quarter of the orchards with French vinifera grapevines. "It wasn't long before we decided there are more wine drinkers than cherry pie eaters," Roberta explains why she and Joanne ventured into grape growing.

Roberta and Joanne sold their grapes for more than a decade until Roberta realized their potential in the wine business. "We sold grapes to local wineries first, and they were winning medals with the fruit." In 2000, the two friends opened Michigan's first exclusively women-owned winery, Chateau de Leelanau.

While Chateau de Leelanau holds an impressive track record of awards and customer success, Roberta is quick to credit her team. She sought winemakers John Fletcher and Vera Klokocka after learning of

their reputation in British Columbia, Canada. Both had a significant impact on the Canadian wine industry.

Vera, one of only three boutique winery owners in British Columbia in the early 1980s, was instrumental in persuading British legislature to adopt a new farm winery act to support small, estate wineries. "I marched into parliament with a loaf of my home-made bread and a case of wine to convince them of the possibilities." Today, the market for Canada's boutique wineries has grown exponentially.

At this same time, John was experimenting with cold-climate grape growing, overseeing regional operations for Canadian wine mammoth Vincor International. He later met Vera when purchasing her Hillside Farm Winery.

After more than a year of retirement, including some travel in Europe, Vera couldn't resist getting back into winemaking. John sold his partnership in his winery and he and Vera created a winery consulting business that served wineries throughout Canada. Roberta heard of the team's legendary partnership and wine "growing" expertise and lured them to Chateau de Leelanau.

The opportunity to apply their winemaking skills in northern Michigan's growing industry—and in its cold climate—had great appeal. "The area has special growing conditions that impart wonderful flavors," John explains. "No one has the same flavors as northern Michigan."

The dynamite team was exactly what Roberta was seeking for the winery. "They're growers who understand our unpredictable climate." While it may have been Roberta's encouragement and the unique growing conditions that brought John and Vera to the area, it is because of their admiration for the people of Leelanau that they now consider the peninsula home. "We love the people here," says John, "they're nice folks."

The mature vineyard, situated near the tip of the peninsula, grows vinifera varieties like Chardonnay, Riesling, Cabernet Franc, and Merlot, as well as newer vines of Bianca and Regent. Located on the forty-fifth parallel, the area has been a successful fruit-growing region for centuries, but its cold, fickle climate makes winemaking all the more challenging.

"It's like Tara in *Gone with the Wind* … it's the land," Roberta explains. "Mother Nature either shines on you, or she doesn't. When everything connects, it's just astounding."

The team's dynamics are seamless. "Everything is hands-on," John explains. "If we pick today, we process today, to capture the essence of the fruit. From harvest to pressing is three hours."

John also values Roberta's faith in his and Vera's skills to bottle the wine at the absolute perfect moment. "If a wine isn't ready to be released, Roberta supports our decision to cellar it until it's absolutely ready. Don't be surprised to see a new release be a three-year-old vintage. You can't rush the processing."

While touring the vineyard, we tasted a 2004 Cabernet-Merlot blend not yet released, which was absolutely bold and full of interweaving flavors of blackberry, a hint of cherry, and even slight vanilla from its ageing in French oak toasted with vanilla.

You can sample the Cabernet Merlot in the winery's tasting room, conveniently placed on the main thoroughfare through Leelanau Peninsula near five other wineries. The renovated 1949 dairy barn and its gleaming white silos jut into the sky, making it easy to spot along the highway. The rustic and charming atmosphere makes sipping the winery's wines all the more enjoyable.

Tenascent White was honored in 2006 at the Michigan Spirits and Wine Competition, as was the winery's Rose' De Cabernet Franc described as "tasty, bright and focused with apple, pear and strawberry flavors." The limited production Tenascent Red has rich flavors with plenty of toasted oak and traces of berry and plum.

Taste wines and shop for gifts and home décor that include fun wine racks, German stemware, and gourmet dark chocolates—pair it perfectly with the

Cabernet. During the summer months, get a double scoop of Moomer's homemade ice cream to round out your "up north" experience that awaits you at Chateau de Leelanau.

"Enjoying wine is a lifestyle," Roberta concludes. "If you drink a glass of wine each day, it's a known fact that moderate wine drinking and its antioxidants effectively reduce stress." Now that's the doctor's order.

GET IN TOUCH

5048 South West Bay Shore Drive
Suttons Bay
(231) 271-8888
wines@chateaudeleelanau.com
www.chateaudeleelanau.com
GPS: N 44° 54.36438, W 085° 37.95816

Tasting Room:
Frankenmuth
976 South Main Street
(989) 652-3700
GPS: N 43° 19.34178, W 083° 44.44128

Chateau Fontaine Vineyards and Winery

Lucie Matthies has crawled on her hands and knees over every inch of her vineyard—and not just once. Each time a new block of vines is planted, she nurtures them as if they are her children; tending to their every need for four years until she feels they've reached their potential.

When Lucie and her husband, Dan, found their land in 1970, they simply saw it as an escape from fast-paced careers in the ski industry. It wasn't until 1989 when a local vintner asked them if they'd be interested in growing grapes for him did they plant the farm's first vines. "We planted every year and ended up with 24 acres," shares Lucie. "We were always interested in wine and already had these beautiful vineyards, so we decided to make wine ourselves and opened the winery in September 2000."

Lucie and Dan are proud of their farm and its massive rolling hills, covering 90 acres of prime land on Leelanau Peninsula. Today, more than 25 acres consist of grapevines, including their favorite Chardonnay in their "North Point" vineyard and, most recently, Riesling, an increasingly popular Michigan wine. Only the second wine maker in northern Michigan to grow Auxerrois, Dan crafts a delicious wine called Woodland White, produced with the French varietal.

Formerly landlocked by the old railroad, the farm still boasts the 1929 home, a Sears' house kit delivered by railway, as well as a 1909 granary. Lucie's nearly 20-year-old quarter horse, Rose, grazes near the historic structures at the base of the vineyard hills.

Lucie insisted we take home a shirt-hem-full of plums as we passed a

tree loaded with ripe, juicy fruit on a tour of the vineyard.

The French were the first to settle in the area, followed by potato farmers who operated the farm for decades. "A gentleman I met recently told me that he used to roll potatoes down our hills when he was a kid," Lucie fondly shares. With the land's French history and Lucie being able to trace Fontaine, her middle name, back to the early fifteenth century in France, the Matthies' vineyard name, Chateau Fontaine, is truly a tribute to those pioneers.

Lucie's expressive bright blue eyes tell of her hard work and her family's dedication. She gives much credit to her son: "Doug is the very best at caring for the vineyard. He works incredibly hard."

In addition to ensuring healthy vine growth, Doug also fertilizes wild plum trees and blackberry bushes native to the land. Lucie insisted we take home a shirt-hem-full of plums as we passed a tree loaded with ripe, juicy fruit on a tour of the vineyard. "Pop them in your mouth whole and then spit out the pit," she advises. "They're so juicy." Only a few made it home and our mouths still water thinking of them.

Lucie invited us to take a moment to appreciate the 360-degree view of Leelanau Peninsula with faraway landmarks of Ciccone and Boskydel vineyards. At this moment, we truly gained a new appreciation for growing and managing grapevines as the Matthies' workers, led by Jesse, trimmed acres of vines to the catchy, swaying beat of Latin music.

Back in the tasting room, we sampled their very tasty Chardonnay. "It's not a Napa or French Chardonnay; it's a Michigan Chardonnay," insists Dan. "It's less oaky than most, with more fruit aromas." Another

and purple coneflowers to greet new guests. Lucie adds, "The vines need the sun to bake them, while the air goes right through them."

Before you leave, take a peek at their cork-lined bathroom wall, a tribute to the wine consumed by Dan and Lucie over the years. "We started collecting the corks for fun and as a way to remember which wines we loved; showcasing the corks on the wall seemed like a fun, decorative idea." You can spot a Chateau Fontaine cork somewhat centered among other corks from the region.

popular wine is the sweeter Cherry Wine, crafted with tart cherries from the region, while red wine enthusiasts are fond of Woodland Red, a blend of estate-grown Cabernet Franc, Merlot, and Syrah.

Through the tasting room's strategically placed window, peer up toward the vineyard. "Rolling, south-facing hills are ideal for growing grapevines," Dan enthuses as he shares a seat with wine dog Nick, an English setter, who jaunts up and down the outdoor walkway lined with red-tipped daisies

GET IN TOUCH

2290 South French Road
Lake Leelanau
(231) 256-0000
dlmatthies@aol.com
www.chateaufontaine.com
GPS: N 44° 56.8683, W 085° 45.28134

Cherry Republic Winery

A bold market position proclaiming North America as the Cherry Republic unknowingly launched an empire of more than 160 cherry products. Proprietor Bob Sutherland boasted Cherry Republic as "the land of life, liberty, beaches, and pie," on a T-shirt design, which he sold out of the trunk of his car while in college in 1989. "I sold 3,500 of those shirts," Bob proudly recalls.

"I've been a little businessman since I was seven years old." While other kids were setting up their lemonade stands, Bob started his entrepreneurial journey with a Petoskey stone stand in front of his home in Glen Arbor. Even back then, Bob understood the importance of pricing and display. "I had 50-cent stones in one bowl and 25-cent stones in another and covered them with water to bring out the color. From that moment, I was a businessman every summer," shares Bob.

The success of his T-shirt sales led Bob to create the Boomchunka cookie, Cherry Republic's first-released and oldest product. The Boomchunka is a delicious cookie with no preservatives made with dried cherries, white chocolate, and rolled oats. "We've probably sold 750,000 over the last 15 years," says Bob.

Diversity is the key to Bob's success, not only in his product line, but also his modes of distribution. "Having a retail outlet is great," says Bob, "but around here everybody goes home in the winter." Bob created a snazzy and effective catalog early on, which he later expanded to the Internet.

75

One wine we encourage you to take home is Conservancy, a refreshing, full-flavored wine made with 100 percent locally grown Balaton and Montmorency tart cherries.

Today, Bob's products are available in his Glen Arbor headquarters store, at several retail locations across the country, over the telephone using his catalog, and online through the company's web site. Cherry Republic has a vast distribution to over 300 retail outlets across the United States and to over 50 countries around the world.

From the Cherry Republic T-shirt to the Boomchunka cookie to an expansion of 150 additional cherry products, Bob is a master at diversifying his product line. His most recent endeavor, Cherry Republic Winery, opened in 2004, serving specialty wines produced from cherries, of course.

The family-friendly tasting room is surrounded by a dog-friendly porch. The official "Dog Bar" sign invites your canine friends to "belly up to the bar" where a refreshing bowl of water awaits. You're invited to lounge on the porch as well, or wander inside to enjoy wines while your children, or friends who favor non-alcoholic beverages, choose a favorite flavor of Boomchuggalugga Soda Pop, named one of Oprah Winfrey's "Favorite Things" in 2005.

One wine we encourage you to take home is Conservancy, a refreshing, full-flavored wine made with 100 percent locally grown Balaton and Montmorency tart cherries. Help preserve northern Michigan's farmland by purchasing some, as $1.00 from every bottle sold goes toward the Leelanau Conservancy.

Walk a few steps to the Great Hall Retail Store after wine tasting. The barn-style building is where you can sample diverse cherry products. Take home a bag of your favorites, or order gift packages boxed in the unique Cherry Republic style with natural wood shavings and pine cones. Stroll over to the bakery and café for pastries, ice cream, or Sunday brunch with freshly brewed coffee on the outdoor patio. Visit in the summer to challenge your skills at cherry pit spitting and cherry stomping. Movies and musical entertainment are also frequent summertime features.

Test your stomach muscles with the Boomchunka Monster Sundae, made with two Boomchunka cookies, five scoops of your choice of ice cream, and all the toppings you want. If you finish the delectable dessert, you get your photo proudly displayed on the wall along with all the others who have mastered the task. Otherwise, join other sundae underachievers with a headshot on the "hall of shame."

Salute the trunk of a car artistically attached to the Great Hall's exterior wall and symbolic of Bob's humble "trunk" beginning and achievement in creating an "everything cherry destination." The mature pine setting, natural rock sidewalks, and timber buildings framed by wild flowers and colorful poppies provide the perfect setting for you to experience what Bob deems, "the greatest of all the fruit"—the cherry.

GET IN TOUCH

6026 South Lake Street
Glen Arbor
(800) 206-6949
info@cherryrepublic.com
www.cherryrepublic.com
GPS: N 44° 53.79498, W 085° 59.34024

Ciccone Vineyard & Winery

An **Italian heritage influences** Silvio "Tony" Ciccone as he fulfills his lifelong dream to establish a vineyard in northern Michigan. A descendant from Pacentro, located in the Abruzzo region of Italy, he was first exposed to winemaking by his parents. "We had wines on the table all the time," reminisces Tony, the youngest of six boys.

Tony and his wife Joan carried on the family tradition of making wine while working in the auto industry and raising eight children, including daughter and pop star Madonna. He grew his first vineyard on a half-acre lot in the backyard of his Rochester Hills home. "I had a mix of grapes; some of my dad's Zinfandel vines, some hybrids, and some European vinifera," says Tony. Over the years, Tony experimented with wines for family and friends, honing his winemaking skills.

As Tony was approaching his retirement from General Dynamics, his desire to establish a vineyard only grew stronger. Tony began looking for property around the Traverse City area as it had been a favorite vacation destination for the Ciccone family. A hillside property with quality growing conditions and a landscape view of the surrounding valleys and bay beckoned him. In 1995, Tony and Joan planted their first vines and opened Ciccone Vineyard and Winery in 2001 atop the hills of Suttons Bay.

A beautifully renovated 1937 stately red barn sits amid the grapevines. Tony renovated the barn, which today is used for weddings and other special events. Large windows that swing open bring in the natural

Tony and Joan are often seen around the estate providing the necessary grunt work that goes into operating a winery, from tending the vines to serving wines at special events.

breeze from Grand Traverse Bay and provide one of the area's most majestic views.

"We have beautiful sunrises and sunsets," describes Tony, "and the view is beautiful in both directions. Artists come up all the time and sit on the hillside and paint. It's great to see them out there."

Tony and Joan are often seen around the estate providing the necessary grunt work that goes into operating a winery, from tending the vines to serving wines at special events. As we were lucky enough to be part of the Ciccone's first wedding held on the property, as bride and bridesmaid, we can attest to the magical backdrop of Grand Traverse Bay and the wonderful wines for toasting.

You can sample the estate-grown wines in the peaceful ambiance of the tasting room boasting European elegance, intricate antiques, and a beautiful fireplace, or on the back patio under plenty of shade. A focus on handcrafting high-quality reds is balanced with the production of several whites, including their popular Gewürztraminer, which has won numerous awards.

Taste the Pinot Noir with light aromas of ripe berries and oak and the Cabernet Franc, a medium body red exhibiting earthy flavors of green pepper, black olive and clove. A proprietary wine, Pallino Red, is named for the ball used to play bocce ball. The label features a fun photo of Tony throwing a pallino on his seventy-fifth birthday.

For something unique, try their Dolcetto, a favorite for its complex, pure flavors. Tony is the first to grow and produce Dolcetto in Michigan. "I believe I'm the only one producing Dolcetto east of the Mississippi," Tony informs us. It is the principal grape grown in the Piedmont region, where it is considered a favorite everyday wine of northern Italy.

We've since learned that Madonna is not the only dancer in the family, as Tony shares a story about Joan and two of their other daughters, Melanie and Jennifer. "Melanie was visiting from California and decided she wanted to crush grapes with her feet, the traditional way. They turned on Italian music and all three started dancing in the grapes."

Noteworthy is a release of a limited edition Madonna label. Tony details, "There are five different designs on the labels from Madonna's *Confessions on a Dance Floor album*. We have a Cabernet Franc, a Pinot Noir, a Pinot Grigio, a Chardonnay, and a Gewürztraminer, all from the 2005 vintage."

Tony is proud of his daughter's eleventh album. He shares that the wines are in honor of "our favorite disco queen going back to her dance floor roots." Each label consists of an artistic photo of Madonna and boasts the signatures of both Madonna and Silvio T. Ciccone. If you're lucky enough to get your hands on one of the limited collectable bottles, you can expect to grab them for $40 per bottle.

GET IN TOUCH

10343 East Hilltop Road
Suttons Bay
(231) 271-5553
cicconewines@aol.com
www.cicconevineyards.com
GPS: N 44° 54.41388, W 085° 38.91822

Gill's Pier Vineyard & Winery

Antique lovers will delight in the treasure trove to be discovered within Gill's Pier Vineyard and Winery's understated pole barn exterior. Its simplicity is quite fitting as proprietor Kris Sterkenburg shares, "We built our tasting room around the pieces we've collected."

Kris and her husband and coproprietor, Ryan, love antiques. "My parents used to take us antiquing as kids—of course, I hated it then," Kris laughs. It was on vacation in Europe with her mom, dad, and sister when she fell in love with the magnificent, mahogany doors that now welcome you into their private tasting room accented with wooden grape presses and an inviting fireplace. Kris tells us that the doors' provenance is tracked to a Belgian monastery, where she envisions they opened into a room where monks brewed ale to fund their work. The monastery was destroyed and rebuilt four times; the doors eventually ended up in an antique shop in London.

The most notable antique, for its size alone, is the pristine-conditioned 1936 Ford stake truck that, depending on the time of year, may be positioned outdoors and decorated with seasonal displays, or indoors holding fun and sophisticated home accessories and wine-related gifts. "It runs like a charm," Kris confides. The tasting room's built-in garage door easily accommodates the truck's indoor/outdoor uses.

The gleaming polished walnut floor reflects the overhead antler and teardrop glass chandelier adding soft light to the richly hued interior. The spacious

With the investment of a new winemaking facility, the Sterkenburgs look forward to continuing their focus on producing high-quality, boutique wines.

Daily's was owned by a man named Kern Daily who was rumored to often say, "You don't get much; it doesn't cost much; and it doesn't take long to eat." The fare of the day was often fresh baked beans and rolls for 25 cents. The bar, believed to have been salvaged from the restaurant, eventually made its way to Kris by way of her uncle, an avid antiques collector, who shipped the heavy bar to Kris and Ryan in three pieces.

The reassembled, stately bar is where you'll sip smooth, tropical Semidry Riesling, or other customer favorites such as Icebox Apple made from a blend of apples and "old-world Bordeaux-style" Merlot with hints of black pepper, black raspberry, and cherry aromas. Support the Leelanau Land Conservancy with the purchase of Houdek Dunes Whitewater, a semisweet blend of Vignoles and Traminette grapes, also notable for its gold medal won at the International Eastern Wine Competition. In addition, Gill's Pier was mentioned in renowned wine writer Tom Stevenson's *2007 Wine Report* as one of the top 10 up-and-coming producers in the Atlantic Northwest Region.

With the investment of a new winemaking facility, the Sterkenburgs look forward to continuing their focus on producing high-quality, boutique wines. A Port Wine made with local grapes and aged brandy, a Cabernet Franc/Merlot blend made from estate grapes and grapes from another Northport vineyard, and a Pinot Grigio are newer additions to the tasting menu.

mahogany bar where you'll taste Gill's Pier elegant and delightful wines has a rich history as well. The Sterkenburgs share the story that was told to them about their tasting bar: it is believed the bar was situated in Dailey's Bar and Restaurant in Long Lake, New York, in the Adirondacks until the 1940s.

Ryan and Kris's love for Leelanau Peninsula is evident in their return to Michigan after living in Wisconsin for many years and in the planting of thousands of grapevines atop their hillside ridge in 2002. The Sterkenburgs opened their tasting room in 2003, paying homage to the bohemian community of Gill's Pier that existed in the region in the late 1800s to early 1900s and consisted of a handful of houses, a post office, and a general store.

In 2006, they added a lovely pond, paving stones, and patio where you're invited to relax and savor the area's quiet beauty. This new outdoor venue was specifically designed for special events and weddings while built to blend in naturally with their estate. Kris and Ryan have teamed with an event coordinator, who can assist with all the details of your intimate event.

Ryan and Kris pay tribute to history through their elegant, antique-filled interior and transport you back to a time where life's simple moments, like sipping handcrafted wines, are intensified.

GET IN TOUCH

5620 North Manitou Trail
Northport
(231) 256-7003
info@gillspier.com
www.gillspier.com
GPS: N 45° 3.57888, W 085° 41.80308

Good Harbor Vineyards

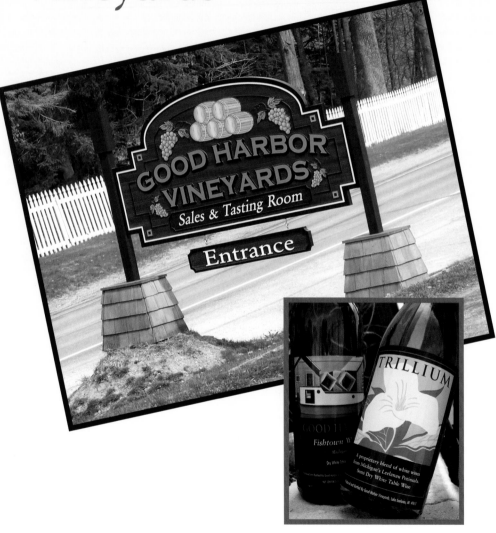

Bruce Simpson is passionate for farming, growing fruit, and for educating others on how he grows his grapes and produces his wines. Veer right when you enter the tasting room and you may catch Bruce testing his wine's readiness with a quick barrel sample, as we did during one of our visits. The overlook provides the perfect opportunity to watch Bruce and his team in action while signs provide the steps for winemaking—a great way to learn about wine in a non-intimidating environment.

Bruce began farming at age five under the guidance of his father and grandfather. They taught him that each fruit has unique needs and to apply techniques to help each type of fruit grow well. He tended acres of cherry and apple orchards on the family farm, getting a lot of hands-on practice growing fruit before heading off to college to study grape growing and winemaking.

Viewing the wine business as a natural agricultural progression to the family enterprise, he added grapevines to the farm in 1978 and two years later opened Good Harbor Winery, named for the nearby harbor. Bruce's strong focus on viticulture and detail to the growing process is apparent in the outcome of the crisp, clean wines he produces. Notably, he is focused on developing a healthier organic mix in the soil and is teaming with Michigan State University on several research projects and test plots.

The bright, clean winery and tasting room are located just south of the historic fishing village of Leland, or Fishtown, a favorite destination for shopping, loading up on fresh fish, and dining at local restaurants. The Simpson family farm is a staple in the region and a lovely hillside accent with mature cherry orchards and a frog-filled pond.

It's apparent the moment you walk through the doors that it's all about the wine, as you'll be immediately drawn to the vibrant display of bottles in open crates along the walls. Colorful labels, created by local artists including Nell Revel Smith, grace the wine bottles, several of which honor local highlights: Fishtown White, Manitou, and Good Harbor Red.

Bruce quickly credits his wife, Debbie, for the alluring display and shares her label-design technique: "It's easier to see artwork you like and then ask the artists if they would like to see their work on a bottle, rather than work with a designer to try to get what you like." It's evident by the presentation of their large selection of wines and the bright, eclectic labels that Debbie excels in this role. Even Debbie's grandmother, Edith Belle Taylor, has a label on the Pinot Grigio Reserve flaunting her artwork.

"Quality, affordable wines" is Bruce's mantra, and you'll find a large variety to sample. Although Bruce prefers drier wines himself, such as Pinot Grigio or Chardonnay, he crafts several sweet wines as well. Perhaps his most popular wine is Trillium, a perennial blend of Riesling, Vignoles, and Seyval with a refreshing, crisp finish. Trillium was introduced in 1984 with the familiar Michigan wildflower on its label.

Other wines to enjoy include the Fishtown White, a blend of Chardonnay, Seyval, Vignoles, and Pinot Gris, and Harbor Red, a rich blend of Pinot Noir, Maréchal Foch, and Chambourcin. Another must-try is Moonstruck, a clean, delicate blend of 60 percent Chardonnay and 40 percent Pinot Noir méthode champenoise cuvee.

The newest item added to the farm's products is a hard apple cider. "The label has a fancy drawing by a local lady featuring an Adam and Eve scene with falling apples," describes Bruce. Making hard cider is a great outlet from winemaking for Bruce as he states, "It's a fun product."

Cap off your visit with a hike up the hill for a glorious view of the Manitou Islands off Lake Michigan's Good Harbor Bay.

Bruce tests wine readiness with a barrel sample.

GET IN TOUCH

34 South Manitou Trail
Lake Leelanau
(231) 256-7165
winery@goodharbor.com
www.goodharbor.com
GPS: N 44° 58.9485, W 085° 46.48638

L. Mawby Vineyards

Sparkling wine producer Larry Mawby is a provocative, bold marketer who has carved a solid niche in the sparkling wine industry. When you visit his tasting room and vineyard, you may be surprised when you meet the laid-back, longtime farmer.

We encourage you to shed any reservations at the door. With sexy monikers like US and Fizz, Larry's sparkling wines are a natural aphrodisiac. What's more, after a few tastings of bubbly you might just be tempted, as we were, to settle in on Larry's outdoor patio overlooking his 13 acres of vines and within view of Ciccone Vineyards atop the hill. You're encouraged to show off your artistry using chunky, colorful chalk. "We want everyone to let loose a little," Larry quietly grins.

This is even more evident by his renowned under-the-white-tent picnics, catered by local chefs and hosted by Larry during summer months. "Reserve your spot early once we post our dates online," advises Larry. The picnics feature different themes, all beginning with sparkling wine, followed by three to five delectable courses and a guided walking tour through the vineyard.

Larry is the creative genius behind the tent picnics and his top-selling brands, Sex and Blanc de Blanc. Poetic descriptions of his wines can also be attributed to Larry, who applies his writing skills finessed years ago while earning an English degree at Michigan State University. Soon after, he settled in Leelanau Peninsula and planted his first vines in 1973, opening his tasting room five years later.

"You can drink bubbly any time, every day, for any occasion," the winemaker states as a matter of fact.

Larry's passion for growing was nurtured on his family's former apple and cherry farms in Rockford, Michigan, and on Leelanau Peninsula. After college, Larry opted to return to farming. "I was interested in doing something that could convey the produce of the land to the table; wine seemed like a natural choice." Larry shares that he also found grape growing appealing, as "it could be done on a small scale, which I also wanted."

Since foraying into winemaking, the northern Michigan sparkling wine pioneer has created a name for himself and his wines; noteworthy is recognition for his Talismøn in Paul Lukacs' *The Great Wines of America: The Top Forty Vintners, Vineyards, and Vintages in 2006*, and inclusion as one of the best sparkling winemakers in the United States, as noted by *Wine Enthusiast* magazine.

His marketing prowess is evident in his distribution beyond Michigan. "Internet sales are increasing and we're expanding our in-state distribution channels," Larry confides. He's also exporting Blanc de Blanc into Denmark and Sweden and is looking for other international growth opportunities.

"You can drink bubbly any time, every day, for any occasion," the winemaker states as a matter of fact. Even if you're not typically a sparkling wine enthusiast, Larry simply wants you to feel comfortable when visiting his winery and tasting his wines. We can almost guarantee you'll find a favorite among Larry's varied styles of wines, as he crafts them applying two methods for two distinct results with varying degrees of sweetness.

Under Larry's L. Mawby label, wines are crafted using Leelanau Peninsula grapes exclusively, following the labor-intensive méthode champenoise (French for "Champagne method"), where wines undergo secondary fermentation and are often aged for three or more years in bottles imported from Rheims of the Champagne province in France. Blanc de Blanc, largely crafted with handpicked Chardonnay grapes that have been whole-cluster pressed, outpaces his other L. Mawby labels, although each style of wine attracts a following.

M. Lawrence, a brand launched in 2003 and made from grapes grown on "planet Earth," consists of wines that are fermented in stainless steel tanks for a shorter duration than bottle fermentation. These wines are crafted using the cuve close method.

With his feet firmly entrenched in Leelanau Peninsula soil and the sparkling wine market, Larry believes Michigan's wine market has room for new wineries: "More choices mean increased traffic to our wineries. I'm constantly surprised at the number of first-time customers. And, with more wines being produced on the planet than sold, it's an exciting time for consumers."

According to Larry, top-selling Sex, a dryer Pinot Noir–Chardonnay blend, hasn't lost its sizzle since he first unveiled the bold brand. "It's our biggest selling M. Lawrence brand," boasts Larry. After sharing a bottle of Sex with Larry in his vineyard, we stocked up on the sparkling wine for refreshing and fun wedding and anniversary gifts and, of course, for our own drinking pleasure.

Consumer demand, as well as demand by private label customers, prompted Larry to construct a new double-temperature, control-capacity cellar in 2006, adjacent to his tasting room. "We're maxed for space on tank fermentation, although our new cellar enables us to ferment and store more wines in bottles in the traditional méthode champenoise."

GET IN TOUCH

4519 South Elm Valley Road
Suttons Bay
(231) 271-3522
larry@lmawby.com
www.lmawby.com
GPS: N 44° 54.93786, W 085° 39.23556

Sparkling Wine: Why Can't We Call It Champagne?

Although the term *champagne* is used freely when referring to our favorite bubblies, it is technically sparkling wine produced in the Champagne region of France under very specific regulations. When produced anywhere else, it's sparkling wine. Why the confusion? The people of Champagne fought hard to protect the name with which they have successfully marketed their luxurious product. While it's illegal in many countries for vintners to label their sparkling wine "champagne," most U.S. vintners have chosen not to use the term out of respect for the Champagne region. So, does that mean that Michigan's sparkling wines are not as luxurious as Champagne? Absolutely not!

Leelanau Wine Cellars

Omena is a blink-and-you-miss-it town that is now a must-visit destination—whether you choose to arrive by car or boat—for award-winning wines and lakeside dining.

Leelanau Wine Cellars' modern tasting room sits on the shores of Lake Michigan with a small marina for docking boats. Flagstone steps protected by a giant rock wall lead the way to the entrance. Inside, expansive windows provide uninterrupted views of Omena Bay and glorious sunrises. Sand-colored maple beams tower over the massive tasting bar and framed windows while complementing the large fieldstone fireplace for a classic setting that is bright with the reflection of the Great Lake.

The dramatic renovation of this property was done with long-time visitors and the water in mind. Father-and-son team Mike and Bob Jacobson bought the deserted cinderblock building that had been for sale for years, seeing the potential with its bay location and small marina. "My passion is restoration of properties," confides Bob. "When I showed a photo of the property to a friend, he exclaimed 'I can't believe you're buying a gas station!'" The project underwent major renovation before Leelanau Wine Cellars opened its new tasting room in fall 2006.

Bob believes they are offering a truly unique experience with wine tasting in view of beautiful Lake Michigan. The adjacent full-service restaurant, Knot Just a Bar, offers delicious cuisine, balcony seating, and Michigan wine, adding to the location's ambience.

When tackling the renovation it was important to the Jacobsons to remain true to their customers who have enjoyed visiting their winery for decades. "You'll find the same wide selection of wines and pricing and the same great attitude by our team. We'll continue to be the winery that has something for everyone," shares Bob. "Whether you are new to the world of wine or even if you have a sophisticated palate, you will find a wine that is just right for you."

Leelanau Wine Cellars was started by Mike, who, at the time, was an attorney in Grand Rapids. He bought land on Leelanau Peninsula in the 1960s with the idea he wanted to become a part-time farmer. In the 1970s, Mike's intrigue with growing a vineyard and opening a winery grew. "Dad thought it would be neat to make wine," son Bob, and co-proprietor, recalls. Mike opened his first tasting room in 1978 in Traverse City before relocating it to Omena, where a large part of their vineyards remains today.

The two Jacobsons reside in downstate Michigan where they operate a real estate development and construction management company. They rely heavily on their winemaker, Nichole Birdsall, a California native, to run the winery, while day-to-day operations are managed by an on-site general manager. Bob oversees the family's wine venture from a management level, as Mike ensures that the wines on which they built their reputation continue to be produced.

Nichole, a former organic winemaker at Bonterra Vineyards of Mendocino County, California, a

division of Fetzer Vineyards, joined the Leelanau Wine Cellars team in 2007. Her move from the warm California climate to Michigan's colder climate was prompted by the opportunity to join an established winery within a dramatically growing wine region.

Michigan's unique growing conditions with multiple seasons and colder temperatures were also intriguing to Nichole. "The Michigan climate offers a great opportunity to grow and to produce high-quality wines expressive of place," observes Nichole.

Nichole experienced the unique harvest of ice wine for the first time shortly after arriving in Michigan. "My first vintage of ice wine was in 2007," states

"Perhaps the most beloved label is the one gracing the Strawberry wine…".

strawberry wine is a little girly, but they usually like it after they try it," laughs Bob. Bruce tends to his strawberry fields in Lake Leelanau, often wearing his favorite shirt shown on the wine label; the picture was painted more than 15 years ago by local portrait artist Fred Petrosky.

Visitors also love the Tall Ship Chardonnay, semi-sweet Winter White, and seasonal Witches Brew, a top-secret red blend with dabs of cinnamon, nutmeg, and cloves. Warm it up in a crock pot and serve the brew in your favorite mug with a cinnamon stick on cool autumn days. Cranberry is a wine to serve at Thanksgiving, while Great Lakes Red, made with Concord grapes, tastes like your favorite grape juice.

A showpiece of Leelanau Wine Cellars is the Meritage, a blend of Cabernet Sauvignon, Cabernet Franc, and Merlot described as full-bodied red aged in French oak barrels. The Select-Harvest Riesling is a constant award-winning wine.

Another award-winning wine is the winery's Vignoles, a hybrid white grape variety, which took home the Gold and Best of Class at the prestigious Pacific Rim International competition in 2006. Notably, the Pinot Noir won bronze at the same competition.

In the vineyard just up a side road from the lakeside tasting room, the Merlot vines flourish, producing a wine worthy enough to be honored as one of America's top 30 new Merlot releases in Wine and Spirits magazine's October 2006 issue.

Nichole. "Ice wine harvest is very interesting. The grapes need to be frozen, and it's very stressful on the vines and quite a risk. I was constantly checking the weather to harvest at the exact moment to conserve the quality of the fruit." Fortunately for us, Nichole timed it just right, producing a delicious Winter Harvest Riesling sure to please the sweeter palate.

Many of the winery's wine labels are charmingly and colorfully presented. Perhaps the most loved label is the one gracing the Strawberry wine, featuring local strawberry farmer Bruce Price. "Some men think the

Leelanau Cellars' Michigan Merlot was described in the magazine as "Light and incredibly pleasant to drink, this has Beaujolais-like scents and flavors of fresh raspberries." The wine label features the artwork of local photographer and painter Malcolm Chatfield, in the form of an acrylic-on-wood painting of Leelanau Peninsula.

The winery's production has quintupled over the past seven years, making Leelanau Wine Cellars one of the largest wineries in the state with nearly 100,000 cases annually. This significant jump in demand prompted the Jacobsons to invest in the bay property. Busting at the seams at the old winery, it was also necessary to expand its winemaking capabilities. The Jacobsons acquired a building in Northport previously owned by Northern Michigan Fruit Company, which is now home to their 37,000 square-foot winery.

A 75-acre vineyard site located on highway M-204 hosts 40 acres of vines referred to as the 204 Vineyard. Planted in the vineyard are acres of Riesling and Sauvignon Blanc grapes, which we spotted for its upward-growing vines. We learned that the healthiest shoots are selected at two years maturity and crossed on the wire to keep them growing vertically. This labor-intensive method assures only the best fruit thrives and is eventually picked to produce a citrusy, dry white wine. The same approach was used to start the Riesling vines a few years ago.

To meet growing demand, look for Gewürztraminer within the next couple of years, once the new vines reach maturity. "I'm excited about having Gewürztraminer come into production," shares Nichole, who enjoys working with varietals that thrive in Michigan.

Applying her California-learned practices to Michigan has helped Nichole successfully craft a wide selection of well-balanced wines that pair well with food. This means that the Jacobsons, combined with Nichole's skills, can continue to produce "quality wines at a good price."

It's all about the water, though. "The water is the reason fruit grows here. Water is the reason we're here and why others come here," Bob succinctly concludes. Michigan wine with a lake view; it can't get any better.

GET IN TOUCH

5219 West Bay Shore Drive
Omena
(231) 386-5201
info@leelanaucellars.com
www.leelanaucellars.com
GPS: N 45° 3.54666, W 085° 35.23758

Knot, Just A Bar

Follow up your wine tasting at Leelanau Wine Cellars with great food at Knot, Just A Bar, a few steps outside the front door of the tasting room. Hamburgers and spicy hot wings, pasta, and fresh catch from the Great Lakes are just a few of the menu items that have made this watering hole a favorite

We're told by Jim Davis, vice president of Epoch Restaurant Group, that "you can expect several Michigan wines on the menu." Indeed, their featured food options may evolve to complement wines produced by Leelanau Wine Cellars. Ale enthusiasts are welcome, too. Sign up for the 69 Beer Club and get your name stenciled on the wall after consuming all 69 of Knot's beer offerings, "over time, of course," Jim laughingly clarifies.

Take a seat on the balcony where you can relax and enjoy a warm bay breeze with a glass of wine and the Boat House salad, enjoy a cool lemonade or ale with the Chargrilled Top Sirloin; or start your day off right with eggs and coffee over a Lake Michigan sunrise.

Longview Winery

"Take the long view" is the response winemaker Alan Eaker gave to his wife Linda Ackley-Eaker, when she said, "You're the right guy in the wrong place." The two met at a conference and resided in different states at the time, where they were each raising a son. Their long-term gamble paid off, though, with a newfound life on Leelanau Peninsula and a winery named for their "long view" commitment made years before.

Linda was the first to fall in love with the deserted dairy farm she discovered on the peninsula. A sculptor, Linda had an eye for seeing beauty in the worn, run-down farm that beckoned her as a place where she and Alan could enjoy their lives together.

So when Alan proclaimed his love to Linda one day, claiming he would do anything for her, she quickly asked if he would buy her a farm on Leelanau Peninsula. Alan, an art professor for 35 years at the University of South Florida, readily agreed with, "Sure! But where is Leelanau Peninsula?"

After the papers were signed to purchase the farm in 1998, Alan finally had his first look at the 100-acre property. "I fell to my knees," he confides. "The property was overgrown and the house was a disaster."

Alan and Linda have made several improvements to the estate they now call home as they literally raised the house up off the ground to add a master suite. In 1999, they planted 10 acres of grapevines to supply local vineyards, taking the "long view" to crafting their own wines. Since that first planting, they've

Cap off your visit with the romantic, nominally priced tasting of Alan's Cherry Port and sweet Winter Ice with a specially made chocolate truffle.

discovered that grapevines thrive in their clay soil, as the water is captured within, giving a constant and natural resource to the vines. "We have a dry farm that never needs to be irrigated," describes Alan, who tends to the vines.

Today, the surrounding mature vines flourish as Alan and Linda continue to improve their beautiful abode. Wine dogs Dora, a large Bracco Italiano, and Merlin, a Miniature Cream Dashschund, bounce around the estate providing a very warm welcome to visitors of the Eakers.

Alan opened Longview Winery in 2005 and established a tasting room in Cedar. Their wines are estate-grown on their private vineyard and poured in the tasting room in one end of an angled, white-painted log cabin built by Linda and Alan.

Alan is passionate about producing "well-polished wines" that reflect the characteristics of the vintage season. He gives fellow winemaker and winery consultant Shawn Walters much of the credit for his award-winning first vintage: "Shawn is simply brilliant."

Before even opening its doors, the winery won Gold honors for its Cherry Port and sweet Winter Ice wine at the 2006 Great Lakes Wine Competition. Only a few months after opening, Longview Winery took home the coveted Judges Special Award at the 2006 Michigan Wine and Spirits Competition for its Cabernet Franc, as well as numerous other country-wide awards.

Enjoy Alan's Rustic Red and Rustic White, which he touts as capturing "the vineyard in the bottles." Rustic White is a fruity, dry wine made with Cayuga grapes that Alan says is done in the spirit of "Vino da Tavola" (Italian for table wine). The Rustic Red, aged in French oak, represents his winery's warm, earthy appeal. Made with estate-grown Frontenac grapes, Alan suggests pairing it with pork loin or grilled steak.

The winery's Cherry Mead is made with fresh honey from a neighboring beekeeper. A touch of cherry from another neighboring farmer resonates as the thick, smooth wine goes down. Enjoy a taste of Alan's "nectar of the gods" anytime of the day as Alan claims you can "drink it as an after-dinner drink or with your morning waffles."

Cap off your visit with the romantic, nominally priced tasting of Alan's Cherry Port and sweet Winter Ice with a specially made chocolate truffle. While you might feel this experience captures the essence of romance, Alan boasts, "All of our wines are romance wines." Rest assured, you'll leave feeling lighter on your feet, ready to embark on a new romantic journey.

If you have the time, it's worth trying to catch Linda in action, fire-bronzing commissioned sculptures in her studio. The renowned artist is known for her work designing the Athena Award statuette and, displayed on the grounds of Michigan State University, the life-size statue of a driving force in horticulture, Liberty Hyde Bailey.

Afterward, stop in the smoke-free, family-friendly Cedar Rustic Inn, open from breakfast through dinner for delicious, American fare prepared by Chef Aaron Ackley, Linda's son and a graduate of the Culinary Institute of America. Wrap up your visit relaxing on the inviting, knotty pine love seats gracing the impressive covered porch.

GET IN TOUCH

8697 Good Harbor Trail
Cedar
(231) 228-2880
info@longviewwinery.com
www.longviewwinery.com
GPS: N 44° 51.216, W 085° 47.59692

Cedar Rustic Inn

Chef Aaron Ackley, a graduate of the Culinary Institute of America, and wife Nikki offer a truly personable, family-friendly dining experience that is topped off with delicious fare at the Cedar Rustic Inn, located in the same building as Longview Winery.

Open for breakfast, lunch, and dinner, Cedar Rustic Inn offers traditional American dishes prepared fresh with local produce from area farmers at prices ranging from $9 to $16 per entree. Love pot roast? Try the crowd favorite Hudson Valley Pot Roast. "It's slow-roasted, choice chuck braised in red wine with root vegetables," describes Aaron. The famous Cedar dog is also a hit with fans of the American classic hot dog.

After a warm welcome from Nikki, we dined at one of the comfy, custom-built walnut dining booths, savoring gourmet Rangoons, fresh house salads, and Parmesan-crusted whitefish—delicious meals leaving us with the desire to return soon to experience more of Aaron's tasty foods. We plan to time our next visit over a long summer day, so we can kick back on the outdoor patio over seasonal, fresh dishes (213) 228-2282.

Cherry Mead

Mead is a smooth beverage crafted from honey and water, believed by some to be the first alcoholic beverage. Getting its origins before anyone can recall, mead was enjoyed by ancient Greeks and Romans and was believed to be the popular drink of medieval times. While mead is not a well-known beverage in the United States today, a newer version, Cherry Mead, is an even more unique product. Longview Winery is the state's first winery to produce the smooth, mulled wine made from fermented cherry juice and honey. Stop by Longview to experience the world's oldest drink for yourself.

Raftshol Vineyards

A century-old farm has been home to three generations of Raftshols who have earned a living from the land, each with a different agricultural focus. A dairy farm, a cherry orchard, and now a vineyard, the farm has played a vital role in Leelanau Peninsula's farming roots and in carrying forth a multigenerational work ethic.

Raftshol Vineyards is tucked roadside along a winding thoroughfare on the sunrise side of the peninsula. A stately, old weathered post-and-beam barn, built by grandfather Anders Raftshol in 1906, may first catch your eye; however, very quickly you'll be drawn to the charming sign welcoming you to their tasting room, which opened in 1999.

An attractive vintage photo of a 20-year-old Jean Raftshol graces the sign. A former economics teacher in Northport, Suttons Bay, and Leland, she very wisely instilled pride for farming and living off the land in her two sons. Today, brothers Warren and Curtis continue the family tradition with Raftshol Vineyards and honor their mother by featuring her photo on their wine labels as well.

The dairy farm was established by Anders, who raised cattle until 1930. Warren and Curtis's father, Karl, converted the farm into cherry orchards. More than four decades in the cherry business, about three decades of which were prosperous, ended when the orchards were pulled in 1975 as the cherry industry was struggling. Grapevines were planted in 1985, when Warren returned to the family farm after studying music in Hollywood and earning a master's degree from Northwestern University.

Warren's firsthand knowledge of the land in which he grew up inspired him to plant red vinifera grapes on the peninsula, which he now attributes to "recklessness." It was initially believed by local growers that red grapes would not grow in the cold climate. He proved them wrong, but still advises others before planting the reds in Michigan, "Look before you leap. It certainly has its ups and downs."

Today, 12 acres of mature vines grow four red varietals including Cabernet Franc, Cabernet Sauvignon, Merlot, and Pinot Noir, and three white varietals including Chardonnay, Riesling, and Gewürztraminer. Warren grew grapes for several years before tackling the wine business; as he recalls the decision, "Making wine seemed more interesting." He also felt that it was a logical move as did Curtis, an airline pilot, who partnered with him to start the winery.

With a focus on Bordeaux-style reds—a much different tactic than most Michigan wineries—Warren produces Cabernet Sauvignon, Cabernet Franc, Merlot, and Pinot Noir in addition to two red blends, Raftshol Red and Claret.

Their first release, Raftshol Red, is a blend of Cabernet Franc, Merlot, and Cabernet Sauvignon and continues to be their most popular wine, along with their Chardonnay. Claret, a blend of 50 percent Cabernet Franc and 50 percent Cabernet Sauvignon, offers a full-bodied red full of great flavor. Don't miss their light port, named Any Port in a Storm, as Warren claims, "Any Port in a Storm is always a favorite."

You can sample their wines, usually poured by Warren himself, in a simple, low-key building located next to the century-old barn. The tasting room was built after Warren ditched his aspiration of converting the family barn into a tasting room and winery due to excessive renovation costs.

On your travels, you may just run into Warren when he's not in the tasting room, often sporting jeans, suspenders, and a gentle smile. Warren, following his mother's dedicated work ethic, still distributes his wine the old fashion way: he loads up his truck and drives door-to-door, visiting retailers throughout Michigan.

GET IN TOUCH

1865 North West Shore Bay Drive
Suttons Bay
(231) 271-5650
warren@raftsholvineyards.com
www.raftsholvineyards.com
GPS: N 45° 0.52752, W 085° 37.19688

Shady Lane Cellars

Sand-toned and lightly speckled rocks collected from the surrounding farm and possibly from Lake Michigan's nearby shores more than 100 years ago glow spectacularly on bright, sunny mornings. The fieldstone-enveloped chicken coop and grain cellar, dating back to the early 1900s, is the centerpiece of a 100-acre farm that is home to Shady Lane Cellars.

In 1988, nearly 12 acres of cherry, peach, and apple orchards were converted to grapevines of Chardonnay, Pinot Noir, Riesling, and Vignoles with first vintages released in 1992. Three years later the old chicken coop, retaining its original fieldstone, underwent its transformation.

The chicken coop's ceiling was raised and topped off with a gleaming copper roof. The interior was warmed with a granite wine tasting bar and Douglas Fir and Italian tile flooring throughout. Today, softly played, wine country music intensifies the tasting room's comfortable elegance where "come as you are and drink what you like" is the mantra. As wine-maker Adam Satchwell likes to say, "The chickens never had it so good!"

Shady Lane Cellars is the shared vision of Grand Rapids–based Joe O'Donnell and Bill Stouten, hunting and fishing buddies who purchased the farm with the vision of producing northern Michigan wines. After hiring Larry Mawby to get them started with their first few years of vintages, Joe and Bill brought Adam on full time in 2000 as winemaker. Adam is thrilled to see Joe, a neurosurgeon, become more involved in day-to-day operations as Joe gets closer to retirement.

Today, grapes cover 41 acres and include Pinot Grigio, Cabernet Franc, and Merlot specifically grown for blending. Except for additional Riesling grapes needed to meet customer demand for their wildly popular Riesling wines, Shady Lane Cellars intends to be completely self-sufficient by 2008.

We asked Adam how things have changed since he first became winemaker. Adam replied with unbridled enthusiasm, "We're doing everything different, from vine canopy management to fermentation to final processing of the wine."

Adam is particularly excited about his new Pinot Noir Reserve. "It's fruit-driven; bigger, gustier, beautifully integrated, and lightly oaked. We really aim to make a different wine." He has dedicated vines to his reserve wines, believing the more dense the vines, the higher quality Pinot Noir he can produce. His winemaker's skills were sharpened over the years, learning tricks of the trade from others.

Adam fondly recalls his first tasting experience when his parents, avid wine drinkers, served their four sons small tastes of 1949 Chateau Haut-Brion. Adam laughs, "I didn't like it all." His parents assured him with, "Some day you'll understand this."

Odd jobs delivering pizzas, silk-screening T-shirts, and gas exploration that didn't click with Adam prompted him to respond to an ad for a position as a wine clerk in a Kalamazoo wine store just shy of his eighteenth birthday. It was during this year of learning about wine that he said, "Ah-ha. I'm hooked."

Adam headed to California and entered viticulture and enology programs, influenced by his uncle working in northern California's wine industry since the 1960s. While in Santa Rosa, Adam recalls, "I'd save up my beer money and hitch a ride to Mendocino County to help my uncle out on the weekends."

He also worked in a winery along the Russian River in Sonoma County and later followed "Uncle Jed" to Kendall-Jackson when Jed Steele became Kendall-Jackson's first winemaker. A stint as winemaker in the Hudson River region of New York was followed by his return to Michigan, where he managed retail wine sales in Dearborn before hooking up with Joe and Bill. "I've never looked back. I plan to stay here forever," shares Adam.

Shady Lane Cellars' wines show off classic cool climate characteristics of the region with intense aromas and flavors. The popular Blanc de Blancs sparkling wine blends a touch of fruit, toastiness, and spice, while favorite Sparkling Riesling is an "unabashedly fun wine." Notably, Adam's 2004 Semidry Riesling was awarded "Best of Class Gold Medal" against Rieslings from all over the United States in the prestigious San Francisco Chronicle Wine Competition, and the 2005 vintage won "Best of Class" double gold medal at the Michigan Wine and Spirits Competition.

Adam also produces limited production wines, including Late Harvest Vignoles, Cabernet Franc, and other limited-distribution wines. "I like to offer small lots of other fun, interesting wines that are only available in our tasting room."

One of his favorites is the Muscat. When we asked Adam to explain how Muscat tastes—a wine we hadn't enjoyed yet—he promptly replied, "It embarks flavors you never forget. It's real perfumy with lots of personality. I absolutely love dry Muscat."

Adam's enjoyment of a good glass of wine paired with seasonal fare is evident as he continues to speak poetically about Muscat. "My favorite meal, every spring, is fresh asparagus with a lightly poached egg on top. To me, that's spring."

A jaunt out to the vineyard with Adam one early fall morning had him touting the wild leeks grown along the property, another one of his favorite spring meal accents. He also shared his favorite picnic spot; a secluded high point along a two-track behind the most easterly vines and cherry trees. Sunlight peeks through from over Lake Michigan, casting a gentle morning glow through a forest of trees.

Visit Shady Lane Cellars off-season and you're sure to spend an afternoon relaxing in their lovely tasting room, possibly enjoying Adam's Pinot Noir Reserve, one of his Riesling vintages, or his newer Gewürztraminer. Better yet, time your visit to coincide with the winery's seasonal barbeques and you may just find Adam on the back patio ruling over the grill.

GET IN TOUCH

9580 East Shady Lane
Suttons Bay
(231) 947-8865
info@shadylanecellars.com
www.shadylanecellars.com
GPS: N 44° 53.53668, W 085° 39.80166

Willow Vineyard

An unexpected stumble across an old, fallen-down sign more than 25 years ago brought John and Jo Crampton to their "million-dollar view." Touring around the Leelanau Peninsula on a weekend get-away, John and Jo noticed a spectacular view along the main thoroughfare between Suttons Bay and Traverse City. "We pulled to the side of the road," Jo reminisces, "and walked up the side of the hill for a picnic."

After savoring cheese, meats, bread, and wine while basking in the panoramic view, John and Jo were making their way back down the hill, discussing how great it would be to someday live on a property like that, when they unexpectedly stumbled across an object lying in the pasture. "A for sale sign was in the weeds," shares Jo. "It had fallen down and looked like it had been there for years."

John and Jo contacted the owners offering to purchase a quarter of the available land in hopes of eventually building a home. "We just knew we were going to live on it someday," shares Jo.

They relocated to Leelanau Peninsula three years later, leaving behind their fast-paced lifestyle as landscapers in the Detroit area. Their first "up north" home was a 450-square-foot cottage located on Grand Traverse Bay. "We were on the bay," said Jo, "that's all that mattered." The beauty outside their door was worth the small space and other sacrifices, such as not having a staircase, which required them to climb through a small hole in the ceiling to get to their loft bedroom.

John designed all of the buildings on the property including their chalet-style, cedar-shackled home with plenty of room for Jo's shoes. Their slower-paced lifestyle on the peninsula carried over to development of their estate. "It's been baby steps for Jo and me. We have built everything," states John.

The name Willow is in honor of an old willow tree that was located at the end of their drive. "The willow had been struck by lightning and was split in two," explains Jo. Today, the broken willow tree has been replaced with a thriving dwarf pussy willow in front of their tasting room. "It's like Cousin It on steroids," laughs Jo, "it just keeps growing."

John learned the art of winemaking under the tutelage of veteran winemaker and neighbor Larry Mawby, who gave him the confidence he needed to open his business. "I told Larry, 'I'll give you the muscle, if you give me the knowledge.'" Larry agreed and the partnership lasted almost four years, allowing John's first three vintages to be crafted at the L. Mawby winery. Willow opened on a busy Labor Day in 1998, which John recalls with a laugh, "The first day was a little scary for me. I didn't know we had to answer questions about the wine."

The rich growing conditions of their land inspired them to become farmers, but it wasn't until after an evening of drinking wine that they knew their passion was to plant vines and become winemakers. They planted their first vines of Chardonnay in 1992, followed soon after by Pinot Noir and Pinot Gris plantings in their eight acre vineyard.

John and Jo lived in tight quarters together for almost 11 years until they decided they were ready to build their dream home. "It was my shoes that moved us out of there," Jo jokes. With experienced eyes for a beautiful landscape, they immediately envisioned a home that blended with the land. "We wanted it to be stuck in the hill rather than sitting on top and taking away from the view," says Jo.

John's very first foray into winemaking, a 1996 Pinot Noir, was a momentous experience. Giving him reins to experience the joy and tribulations of winemaking, Larry refrained from offering too much advice. After more than a decade of ageing the wine, John and Jo have yet to enjoy a bottle of their first Pinot Noir as the flavors are still so strong. Today, the award-winning Pinot Noir is their signature wine and customers' favorite.

You can sample their estate wines in the rustic, comfortable tasting room, where you'll almost always find John or Jo behind the bar, pouring their Pinot Noir, as well as Chardonnay, Pinot Gris, and Baci Rosé—wines tasting of the natural fruit flavor indicative of John's careful fermentation in French oak barrels.

Take a stroll through the French doors to a cozy courtyard across from their barrel room, or settle in while music sails through the air and soak up the bright blue bay backdrop, often referred to as the million-dollar view. John and Jo, who are proud of their decades' long marriage, recall the first time they met. "I was fishing off King's Island when I got called home for dinner," remembers John. "We think it was a set-up."

John and Jo are living their dreams on a beautiful hillside vineyard in Suttons Bay. "It's magical; the best move we ever made. We get to stay home, and you come to us for our product. It doesn't get any better than that," Jo passionately expresses.

GET IN TOUCH

10702 East Hilltop Road
Suttons Bay
(231) 271-4810
www.traversebiz.com/willow
crampt3630@aol.com
GPS: N 44° 54.39972, W 085° 38.44182

Old Mission Peninsula Wine Trail

OLD MISSION PENINSULA AVA

The meso-climate of Old Mission Peninsula is unique not only in the state of Michigan but probably in the world. Lying on the forty-fifth parallel (like Bordeaux, Milan, etc.), the peninsula stretches 18 miles into Grand Traverse Bay and is only four miles wide at the broadest point. We are virtually surrounded by the 600-foot-deep waters of East and West Bays. It stays cold longer in the spring, protecting us from the late frosts, and warm longer in the fall when we benefit from an extra six to seven weeks of ripening. The rolling hills and lake-effect snow ensure that no Arctic blasts of freezing air will stay around long enough to harm our vines.

Since most of the volatile compounds which give any fruit its flavor are formed during the last few weeks of ripening, warm (not hot!), dry conditions in October are key in creating the fully ripe, unique wines of the Old Mission Peninsula. Our maritime climate in the middle of North America's vast continental climate provides these conditions for us. We get the warmth when we need it most. The fantastic growing seasons provide us with wines that match and even top the best wines of many of the world's more famous growing regions.

— MARK JOHNSON, VINTNER,
CHATEAU CHANTAL

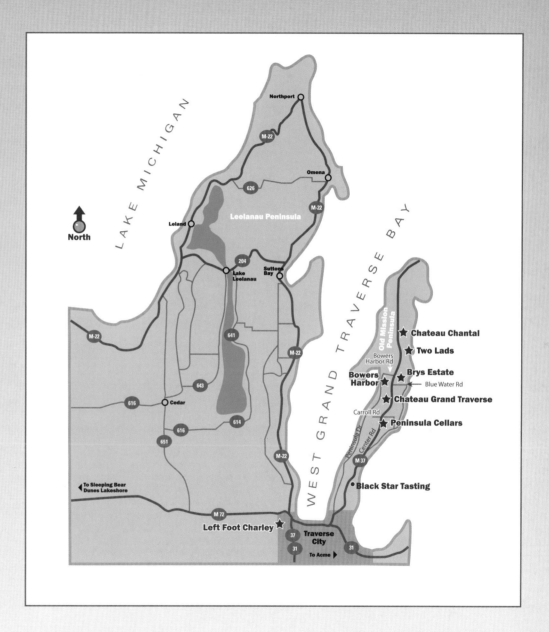

109

Bowers Harbor Vineyards

The first thing you'll notice when you arrive at Bowers Harbor Vineyards may not be the stunning landscape view of the harbor for which the vineyard is named. Rather, your eyes may be drawn to the golf green on the informal "Links at Bowers Harbor."

An official scorecard won't be found, although you're invited to test your golf skills on the mini course with real turf and a few pars, the first of its kind in a Michigan vineyard. The unofficial course isn't the only unique statement you'll find at Bowers Harbor Vineyards.

Winegrower Spencer Stegenga is proprietor of the winery with his mother, Linda Stegenga. The estate stretches over 15 acres of the 43-acre property bought by Spencer's parents in 1985. A lovely, vine-covered portico extending from a former barn that housed quarter horses warmly beckons you to stroll under its flowering greens to the comfortable tasting room.

In 1992, the barn was converted after the Stegenga family planted grapevines on the sloping property, venturing into winemaking in 1990 after "rearing very large cows, sheep, and geese," laughs Linda.

One large animal that is very much a part of today's winery scene is Cooper, the family's Bernese mountain dog. Albeit huge, the gentle giant silently greets guests and can often be seen weaving between customers in the Stegengas' busy tasting room. "He's always on duty," confirms Spencer.

Old Mission's second-oldest winery is also the first to honor its best friends Cooper and the late Otis, an affectionate yellow Lab, on its elegant wine labels gracing sweet, semidry white wines. Spencer isn't sentimental just for his dogs; his prestigious 2896 Langley black label is grown from only his best Merlot and Cabernet Franc grapes in the Langley vineyard. The vineyard was named by Spencer in honor of his grandfather, Harold Langley, who taught him to garden and care for the family's land. The Langley vineyard also produces several acres of Riesling.

Of note, the winery produces "single-vineyard Rieslings," meaning that all the grapes are pulled from one vineyard to create a wine, as Riesling is very terroir-specific, Spencer educates. "A Riesling grown on this slope will taste different from a Riesling grown a mile up the road or from a vineyard several miles down the peninsula." Spencer oversees four winemakers that pull from three single-vineyard Rieslings to craft Bowers Harbor's wines, so you can expect different flavors in each vintage as well as from the different vineyards.

On a golf cart ride through the family's vineyard, Linda pointed out the spot where Spencer asked his wife Erica to marry him. Linda confided that Spencer took Erica by the pond and proposed, boldly stating, "If you'll be my wife, I'll name this vineyard for you." Today, the Erica vineyard produces Pinot Grigio grapes that Spencer has blended with additional Old Mission Peninsula Pinot Grigio grapes to produce his top-selling wine.

"Our Pinot Grigio is our flagship wine. We work very hard to create a first-class, yet comfortable, experience," says Spencer. He indicates this by simple, yet purposeful investments such as using true Pinot Grigio bottles from Italy and placing the label higher on the bottle, so you can see the indented bottom and green tint of the glass.

Spencer also takes grape physiology very seriously, believing the best wines are made by "good quality fruit from the vineyard."

111

patio chair Lake Michigan's Bowers Harbor appears to float atop flourishing grapevines.

One harvest Spencer enthusiastically shared that his team had just harvested nearly 40,000 pounds of Pinot Grigio, to which he added, "I just love the whole aspect of wine and farming. Farming is hard work and a lot of fun. It's truly my passion."

Spencer's personal touch also includes higher-end apparel from Patagonia that can be special ordered in the tasting room with the BHV—Bowers Harbor Vineyard—logo. Spencer believes the combined "touches" strengthen the winery's mission to create for its customers a big experience in "a little place like this."

"We're a world-class, international wine company that's producing wine from northern Michigan," summarizes Spencer before adding that, in the end, "We just want to have fun with the lifestyle."

"Our wine speaks for itself; we capture and enhance what is already there in the fruit," explains Spencer. "We taste the fruit in the vineyard, look at the seeds, feel them in our mouths, and select yeast varieties that further enrich the flavors."

The experience at Bowers Harbor Vineyards can best be savored by relaxing on the inviting patio, accessible through the portico's walkway. On a busy day in October, you can sample new proprietor blends, or find a favorite wine in the tasting room to take outside. Golden, ruby-red, and light green leaves from the canopy of beech and maple trees overhead fall gently around you in autumn, and from your

GET IN TOUCH

2896 Bowers Harbor Road
Traverse City
(800) 616-7615
info@bowersharbor.com
www.bowersharbor.com
GPS: N 44° 53.54466 W 085° 30.94512

Pinot Grigio vs. Pinot Gris: What's the Difference?

Thanks to the movie *Sideways,* most of us have heard of Pinot Grigio, a white grape producing a delicious crisp wine. So, what's the difference between Pinot Grigio and Pinot Gris? They are actually the same grape named differently depending on whether you're Italian or French. In the United States., California typically uses the term Pinot Grigio while other states such as Oregon use Pinot Gris. Then there are states like Michigan who swap the terms back and forth.

Same grape, same flavor? You'll be surprised by the differences between the two as the French and Italian styles of winemaking differ dramatically. Try them for yourself by touring Michigan's wineries on a Pinot Grigio vs. Pinot Gris wine tasting mission.

Brys Estate Vineyard and Winery

In the spirit of adventure and new beginnings, historic doors lead to fresh experiences. Walter and Eileen Brys, owners of Brys Estate Vineyard and Winery, were inspired by arched doorways in Napa Valley and wished to emulate the beauty and simplicity in their winery. In particular, they loved the striking arched doorway leading into an old structure, believed to be a historic horse barn, on Francis Ford Coppola's Californian estate winery.

Wide, mahogany arched doors shipped from Honduras provide the focal point of the gracious fieldstone building housing the tasting bar, vaulted barrel room, and winemaking facility. The arch is repeated indoors in a ceiling that mimics the inside of a half barrel. This unique architectural touch was designed by Walt, who also planned the interior renovation of their 1890 farmhouse and conversion of the tractor barn into a comfortable guest house with the property's grandest view of Grand Traverse Bay.

We are also impressed with the elegant, yet unpretentious, tasting room. The mahogany-lined barrel ceiling complements the elegantly carved tasting bar with raised wooden grape bunches. Raw mahogany from Africa was used by local artisans to handcraft the bar to match a favorite table of Eileen's from Honduras.

In the barrel room, beautiful French oak barrels line the red old-world brick walls. Adjacent to the ageing wine, the gorgeous, maple mid-1800s schoolhouse table centered under a rustic iron chandelier provides an elegant venue for private wine tastings that can be arranged with the winemaker in advance. Just a few

In the barrel room, beautiful French oak barrels line the red old-world brick walls.

steps away from this comfortable room, through tall, six-panel double doors, is a state-of-the-art winemaking facility.

The facility, designed by South African winemaker Cornel Olivier, aided in earning the estate 30 awards in just five competitions. The awards include "Best New Red Wine Discovery" for its Cabernet Franc at the prestigious Wine Appreciation Guild Wine Literary Award Tasting in San Francisco in 2006. Their 2005 Pinot Noir was chosen as "Best of Class" for dry red wine at the 2006 Michigan Wine and Spirits Competition. Both wines have made us unwavering fans as the flavors are smooth, big, and lingering.

Taste both wines at the elegant bar, where you'll also find other dry wines, such as the Signature Red, which is a full-bodied blend of reds, and a lovely, crisp Pinot Grigio. Taking their focus on dry wines a step further, Walt and Eileen offer an ice wine, called, appropriately, Dry Ice.

"Our ice wine is drier than traditional ice wine, with a residual sugar of only 6.7 percent. We present it in an elegant black velvet Brys-embroidered logo tie bag for a perfect holiday gift," shares Eileen.

A trip to Napa decades earlier had planted the seed that someday they would love to own a vineyard. This dream came to fruition after Walt's brief retirement when Eileen fondly recalls, "We thought 'this is not for us'—we were incredibly bored." They almost immediately began looking for land to grow grapes in a community that offered them the lifestyle they were looking for, visiting properties in renowned wine regions, including California, New York, and Texas.

In 2006, Peninsula Township honored the Bryses with a preservation award for restoring the former apple and cherry orchard to a new splendor while retaining the character of the farmland.

Walt and Eileen finally returned to their home state, where, Eileen shares, "Michigan had all of the things we wanted." Walt and Eileen located the old, worn down cherry-farm homestead with great growing conditions and a gorgeous view, as Eileen reminisces, "We looked at this land through rose-colored glasses."

While simultaneously planting 28,000 vines on nearly 25 acres of their new 80-acre farm, Walt and Eileen tackled the renovation of a desolate farmhouse, pump house, and two barns. Today, the gleaming white homestead, encompassing a quaint guest cottage converted from a former tractor and tool shed, looks as if it has been there forever. In 2006, Peninsula Township honored the Bryses with a preservation award for restoring the former apple and cherry orchard to a new splendor while retaining the character of the farmland.

The Bryses have learned from and encouraged Cornel to lead the way in crafting wines during his stay at the vineyard. Raised in Stellenbosch among grapevines and fruit trees in South Africa's wine region, Cornel learned winemaking on his grandfather's farm, before studying viticulture and wine science and apprenticing at area wineries.

Cornel arrived on Old Mission Peninsula through an Ohio State University exchange program as an intern for Chateau Grand Traverse. The opportunity to run Walt and Eileen's new winery enticed the winemaker to join the Brys team. "Cornel led us through two garage-making vintages before our winemaking facility was completed," Eileen remembers.

In early 2007, Cornel left Brys Estate to partner in a new winery. Coenraad Stassen, a fellow South African native and former co-winemaker at Chateau Chantal, took over the winemaking at Brys Estate. Coenraad, who goes by Coen (pronounced "coon"), focuses on high-quality reds and crisp, clean whites. We are looking forward to vintages imparting Coen's elegant style of winemaking using grapes grown in the vineyard. The vineyard consists largely of European varietals, including Merlot, Pinot Noir, Pinot Gris, Cabernet Franc, Gewürztraminer, Riesling, Chardonnay, Chenin Blanc, and Pinot Blanc.

Walt and Eileen's creative side is also reflected in Wally's Wineyard, a second label affectionately named for Walt's ability to easily make people laugh. The easy-to-drink wines, blended from Old Mission Peninsula fruit, boast names of Walt's hunting trophies from the only two times he ever hunted. Hat-wearing Winston, the deer, and cigar-chomping Boris, the wild boar, overlook winery operations, reminding the owners daily not to take themselves too seriously. During our visit and tour, the overhead trophies caught us by surprise and immediately put us at ease, eager to taste their fondly named wines.

Walt describes his "deer" friends' namesakes: "Boris and Winston are patio wines for your summer pleasure while shooting the breeze with family or friends." The third Wally's Wineyard wine, Lucky, was named for the family dog. All three feature catchy quotes, such as "Get lucky at least once a day, doggone it!"

It is evident that Walt and Eileen have embraced the overall spirit of their farm. We appreciate the comfy Adirondack chairs they've set aside for unobstructed views of Grand Traverse Bay. Walk through the welcoming archway for a truly divine experience when you're ready for tasting wines with a local and international flair.

GET IN TOUCH

3309 Blue Water Road
Traverse City
(231) 223-9303
info@brysestate.com
www.brysestate.com
GPS: N 44° 53.03442, W 085° 30.5307

Chateau Chantal

A wandering, winter trek up Old Mission Peninsula's highest ridge on cross-country skis led Bob Begin to spectacular views of Lake Michigan. "Wow! What a vista," Bob remarked at the time. When he learned the property was available, he couldn't believe it. "This panoramic view was for sale," Bob sweeps his arm, recalling. "It was simply pure luck."

Bob and wife Nadine bought the 65-acre cherry farm in 1983 and established Begin Orchards, over time replacing the old cherry orchards with grapevines. Today, 35 acres of vines cover the hillside that wraps around the elegant chalet, Chateau Chantal, named for Bob and Nadine's daughter, Marie-Chantal.

Bob envisioned the old-world experience from the start, "We knew we wanted to build a European-style tasting room with lodging." The winery chateau is truly a destination where you can enjoy an afternoon by their always-lit fireplace, sipping wines and soaking in unparalleled views of an island nature preserve in Lake Michigan through an expansive bay window.

The best way to experience Chateau Chantal is by staying in one of their luxury suites. An executive apartment with a full kitchen, living room with fireplace, two bedrooms and bathrooms, and two private decks provides spectacular views of the vineyards and Grand Traverse's West Bay. Touring the inn, we ran into a lovely bride and her sister getting ready for an evening wedding on the estate. They were thoroughly enjoying their stay in the huge suite. The inn's 10 other elegant and spacious suites offer private whirlpool tubs, fireplaces, and terraces with lake views.

Wine cellar tours, extensive cooking classes, and tapas-style pairing tours round out the seasonal amenities offered, as well an annual fall Harvest Day celebration where brave souls can partake in old-world style grape stomping.

"Feel comfortable and at home here, not intimidated," Bob encourages. He and Nadine wouldn't have it any other way. Indeed, their life has been dedicated to the service of others. Bob was a Catholic diocesan priest for 12 years before heading a construction business. Nadine was a Felician sister and teacher for 22 years.

The welcoming aura of the chateau carries over to exquisite wines crafted by Mark Johnson and assistant winemakers. Mark has been with the Begins from the beginning. A former social worker for the city of Hamburg, Germany, Mark is the third American to graduate from the prestigious wine school, Federal Research Station and Institute in Geisenheim, with a degree in viticulture and enology.

Mark returned to the area after a year-long hiatus from social work turned into a position in winemaking. "I was too hooked to go back," Mark shares. In 1983, the Michigan native returned home to work for Chateau Grand Traverse, where he was the winemaker until he joined Bob's crew.

Panoramic view of Grand Traverse Bay and Power Island.

Coenraad Stassen joined the team in 2003 on an internship through Ohio Sate University and was immediately promoted to assistant winemaker upon completion of the program. The former semipro rugby player acquired his winemaking skills working in South Africa's Cape Town winemaking region. After sharing his skill for making wines "that are easy to drink, but still very elegant," Coen moved to the Brys Estate in early 2007.

119

before wine is stored in 1000-liter "bags in boxes" and loaded on a ship to make the journey north. Final blending and bottling are done on the peninsula. "Malbec often outsells our other comparable reds," confides Bob.

Today, Mark oversees 132 acres of vineyards on the peninsula and produces 30 wines from very dry to slightly sweet. Hot-selling Cerise, a fortified, distilled 100 percent cherry wine can't be kept on the shelf. "We can't label it fast enough," Mark is excited to share. The wine is produced with whole tart Balaton cherries, rather than the more widely used Montmorency cherries. "Balaton is a Hungarian variety that is new to America. It can hang on the tree longer for a darker juice," Mark explains. Naughty and Nice wines, a favorite holiday and special occasion gift set, are red blend varieties. "We wanted to craft red wines for people who don't like red wine," shares Mark. "If you're feeling naughty, enjoy it with fish, or whatever you like. Nice, on the other hand, has a nice balance of sweetness and tannins." Another seasonal favorite is Ice Wine, which has incredible sweetness and fruitiness, "with all the delicateness of a fine Riesling wine."

Other favorite top sellers are Celebrate, a sparkling Chardonnay with a splash of Pinot Noir, and Tonight, a dry "blanc de blanc"—white wine made from Chardonnay. Sweeter palates can enjoy Cherry wine, Gewürztraminer, and Riesling.

"Apples taste like apples, cherries taste like cherries, but grapes taste like the soil."

In the opposite hemisphere from Old Mission Peninsula, Chateau Chantal South consists of 55 acres of vineyards on a 135-acre farm and a winery at the foot of the Andes in Mendoza, Argentina. The investment in the famous region allows Chateau Chantal to offer bigger reds, including Malbec Reserve, a classic dark berry wine with hints of toast, chocolate, and vanilla produced from 43 acres of mature Malbec grapes. Crushing, fermentation, and oak-barrel ageing are performed locally by Chateau Chantal South employees under Mark's direction

Mark educated us on using our sense of smell to best enjoy wine. "There's a reason smells trigger memories; your smell sensory is located next to your memory in your brain. With wine, you enjoy the bouquet, more so than its taste." He demonstrated this for us with a Merlot in his cellar "library" that blended his 1993 and 1994 vintages. The peppery wine was dancing with flavors.

Back in the vineyard, Mark explains, "Apples taste like apples, cherries taste like cherries, but grapes taste like the soil. We like diversity in the land. We want other flavors in the vine, although there's a need for balance to ensure the vine gets the nutrients it needs."

Plump, gorgeous Pinot Meunier grapes caught our eye for their dark color, as well as for the "white hair" on the leaves. Mark explains, "These grapes are the most widely planted in the Champagne region of France. They're well suited for cold climates." The grape's youthful, tart acidity makes a crisp sparkling wine.

Mark's flair for vibrant tasting wines is notable during your visit to Chateau Chantal. Whether a brief stop or weekend stay, you'll love the opportunities to learn about the wines and soak in the breathtaking views and rolling vineyards. As Bob succinctly states, "This is truly a value-added agricultural experience."

GET IN TOUCH

15900 Rue de Vin
Traverse City
(231) 223-4110
wine@chateauchantal.com
www.chateauchantal.com
GPS: N 44° 54.95148, W 085° 30.12978

Experience the Old-World Tradition of Grape Stomping

A bright autumn day bursting with colors of fire and marigold provides the perfect moment to experience the tradition of old-world grape stomping. Thousands of people trek to Chateau Chantal's hilltop for their annual Harvest Day to drink the wine, soak in the sun's rays, and mostly watch brave souls (or is that soles?) climb into the barrel of grapes.

Fearless enough to crush, we tackled this feat with verve, especially after winemaker Mike Johnson taunted us with, "We didn't think you'd show!" And while we had no idea grapes were so cold on bare feet, the desire to partake in a winemaking tradition going back more than a thousand years was too tempting, so we kept on stomping. Experience the old-world tradition for yourself—jump in with both feet and make some vino!

Chateau Grand Traverse

One of the most dramatic views along the Old Mission Peninsula's winding thoroughfare is an overlook where you'll often find motorists and cyclists pulled aside snapping photographs of acres of grapevines that seemingly dip into Lake Michigan's Grand Traverse Bay. The massive, low-lying Chateau Grand Traverse blends naturally with the scenery.

As northern Michigan's oldest commercial winery, Chateau Grand Traverse is owned and operated by Edward O'Keefe Jr., "Ed", along with sons Edward III, "Eddie," and Sean. "I'm an entrepreneur," states Ed. "I come up with the ideas. Eddie is the one who keeps it together, and Sean's the guy who produces the product."

Deemed the "maverick of Michigan wine" in the early 1970s, Ed relishes the role he has played in Michigan's burgeoning wine industry. The Irishman's colorful past illustrates his drive and gustiness. Ed was born in the ghettos of southwest Philadelphia and served in the Korean War. He ended up as captain in the Army's Special Forces before becoming a Federal Treasury Agent with the Federal Bureau of Narcotics in the 1950s.

He attended the Ollerup Gymnastics School in Denmark on a full scholarship. "I made the 1952 Olympics team, but was unable to compete due to a ruptured appendix," Ed reminisces. Afterward, the driven entrepreneur applied his health education degree to owning and operating five extended-care nursing homes.

Ed relied upon the expert advice of Dr. Helmut Becker, the dean of the renowned Geisenheim Oenological and Viticultural Institute in West Germany. He shares that he followed the planting style used in the Rhine region of Germany, applying closer vine spacing and employing a seven-wire parallel trellising system to train vines to grow vertically for more sunlight exposure.

The 1979 harvest bore Riesling, Chardonnay, and Merlot and expanded to include Pinot Noir, Gewürztraminer, and Gamay Noir on 53 acres and has since racked up awards from state, national, and international competitions. In 2006, Chateau Grand Traverse's Ship of Fools, a blend of Pinot Gris, Pinot Blanc, and Chardonnay, won gold in the dry white category at the Pacific Rim International Wine Competition, while the winery's dry and whole-cluster Rieslings won gold medals at two additional international competitions on the east and west coasts.

Today, their vineyards consist of 80 acres of estate vines including Johannisberg Riesling, Gamay Noir, Chardonnay, Pinot Gris, Pinot Meunier, Pinot Blanc, Merlot, Cabernet Franc, and Pinot Noir.

Their vineyard is also home to more than 40 bird species, including, as one bird enthusiast has noted, the rare-to-this-region orchard oriole. Leelanau Peninsula–based Saving Birds through Habitat recognized the O'Keefes in 2006 for their "forward-thinking environmental policies that benefit native birds and plants." Kestrel boxes dot the property; most

In 1974, he packed up his young family and relocated to Traverse City and Old Mission Peninsula to establish the region's first winery. Proud of his father, Sean, who now oversees the winemaking process shares, "My dad moved the whole family up here to make the absolute best Riesling wines."

After reshaping one million cubic yards of dirt into a southwest slope for maximum sun exposure, Ed established the state's first commercial planting of European vinifera grapes. Taking the risky venture very seriously, Ed recalls, "I planted 55 acres the first shot." Until Ed's ambitious undertaking and for years after, it was believed that only more winter hardy hybrid grapes could withstand Michigan's cold climate. Ed proved otherwise.

notably, the boxes surround a small vineyard pond, which is also home to a family of amphibians. The nonprofit bird organization was impressed with the winery's use of organic compost, minimized spraying, and removal of non-native plants from non-vineyard areas to encourage wildlife.

Stay at the Inn of Chateau Grand Traverse, a six-room guesthouse on the property that provides spectacular views, ample bird watching and an easy walk to wine tasting. The 15,000-square-foot guesthouse can be rented in its entirety, or by individual rooms. The spacious, shared space features a formal 18-person dining table and mammoth living room overlooking Grand Traverse Bay. Lounge with a good book in the sunroom, work off indulgences in the gym room, or tour the colossal cellar room, accessible in a "hidden" passage through a secret bookcase.

Sign up for a vineyard and winery tour through their modern winemaking facility, featuring the latest in European technology and winemaking expertise, or take your own leisurely stroll through the vineyards. On your tour, you just may run into Bacchus and ChaBoo, the family's snow-white Samoyed dogs, often seen trailing Eddie, who began working in the vineyard when he was 12.

In his youth, Eddie planted, trellised, and harvested grapes before earning an advertising/marketing degree at Michigan State University. Today, Eddie is president, responsible for day-to-day operations at the winery, as well as distribution. Alongside his father and brother, he is focused on strengthening

the winery's leadership in producing outstanding dry Rieslings, which he calls, "see-through Rieslings."

"A sweet and complex Riesling wine is much like dressing up in a snowmobile suit," Eddie grins. "Whereas a dry Riesling wine is more revealing, much like standing there naked." In a dry Riesling there is very little sugar, which is produced naturally by the fruit, making it more translucent. The winery's Johannisberg Riesling Ice Wine, another of the O'Keefes Riesling offerings, is described as "exquisite with opulent layers of apricot, pineapple, and luscious tropical fruit."

With more than 30 years of focus on producing world-class, mature wines, Chateau Grand Traverse produces more than 30 different wines.

The flourishing, profitable winery with its stronghold in the market wasn't always so. Eddie shared a memorable story of when he asked his father for help with tuition money during his first year of college. At the time, the winery was still struggling to make a profit, so dad Ed, who didn't have the immediate funds available, replied with, "There's always the apple wine" of which there was a plethora. Eddie jammed 32 cases of the wine in his car and sold every bottle to his dorm buddies, paying his semester's tuition with cash the very next day. "It was like a speakeasy," Eddie laughs as he recalls the late night knocks on his dorm room door.

The oftentimes unconventional family runs its winery operations like clockwork while staying connected with its German-influenced roots through younger son Sean and German-born winemaker Bernd Croissant, who has been with the family since 1993.

Fluent in German, Sean attended college at the early age of 16, studying German and Russian literature at the University of Michigan. He later completed his studies in Germany at the renowned winemaking and viticulture school at Geisenheim. The intellectual continues his winemaking education with regular trips to European winemaking regions, most often Germany and Austria, from where he feels northern Michigan wineries have the most to learn.

Sean's "Whole Cluster" Riesling and the "Ship of Fools" Pinot Gris/Pinot Blanc blend are award-winning examples of his adoption of a classic European "minimalist" approach to winemaking. Currently,

Sean's major project is overseeing a newer 30-acre vineyard just north of the winery where he hopes to further raise the bar for Old Mission Peninsula wines through the growing of new Riesling clones, with an emphasis on organic farming.

Bernd, on the other hand, grew up in the renowned Rhine wine region of Germany, where the family's trade was winemaking. Remarkably, his family's history in handcrafting wine dates back to medieval times in 1590. Bernd started as an eight-year-old, cleaning small barrels before learning "whatever it took" to run a winery.

In taking a sabbatical, Bernd decided to move his family to the United States, seeking a life change while gaining additional work experience at a winery. "I initially wanted to go to California where all the grapes are," reveals Bernd, who was subsequently invited to the Old Mission Peninsula by Chateau Grand Traverse through an international work-study program . "I thought 'grapes in Michigan?'" says Bernd, who now treasures the region's growing climate. "The growing season is a little bit shorter than Germany, and a little more challenging. But I don't like to make wines with a recipe, so I like the challenge." The O'Keefes credit Bernd for their many award-winning wines and tremendous growth over the years.

Eddie and Sean's leadership roles are solidly planted in taking the family winery into the future. Even so, Ed isn't planning to retire any time soon—or ever, for that matter. As Ed explains, "I'm good in bad times. My sons are good in good times."

Although disagreeing quite often, the trio feels they make a great team. "If two partners always agree, then one is unnecessary," Eddie grins, recalling the quote he once heard. The O'Keefes never make a major decision regarding the winery until all three of them agree, "or until one of us goes on vacation," Eddie jokes.

With more than 30 years of focus on producing world-class, mature wines, Chateau Grand Traverse produces more than 30 different wines. A second "select" label is produced using grapes from beyond Old Mission Peninsula. Ed built this label as a safeguard against inclement weather that can, in the blink of an eye, destroy a harvest. "I'll never forget the 200 inches of snow we got in the late 1970s," Ed assures. The vintners are now experimenting with new small-production blends, which you can sample in their tasting room.

You'll find yourself in good company with others tasting the winery's award-winning wines, touring the facility on any given day and taking in one of the grandest views of Grand Traverse Bay from the family's vineyard overlook, positioned to give you a picture-perfect backdrop.

GET IN TOUCH:

12239 Center Road
Traverse City
(231) 223-7355
info@cgtwines.com
www.cgtwines.com
GPS: N 44° 51.80742, W 085° 31.1568

Tasting Rooms:
Williamsburg
4160 M-72 East
(231) 938-2291
GPS: N 44° 46.38342, W 085° 29.56284

Onekama
4990 Main Street
(231) 889-0333
GPS: N 44° 21.78966, W 086° 12.16212

Ice Wine: A Labor of Love

Ice wine is a sweet dessert wine crafted from grapes that have been left on the vines to freeze naturally in the cold climate. Once the grapes have been frozen to around 17 or 18 degrees Fahrenheit, they are carefully picked, then pressed immediately to retain the intense concentration of sugar and acidity, resulting in a sweet aperitif.

Ice wine doesn't come easy for the vintner, as it's a gamble every year. The labor-intensive harvest has to survive warm or rainy weather conditions, which may cause the fruit to rot, and avoid birds and other pests who may choose the fruit for their own feast. The rigorous process is a labor of love for Michigan vintners, with the reward of a lovely high-quality, ice-errific product ranging from $35.00 to $80.00 for a 375 ml. bottle. Most ice wines sell out quickly as they are typically produced in small quantities, so grab your bottle today.

Left Foot Charley

Left Foot Charley is winemaker Bryan Ulbrich's alter ego, a nickname fondly given to him by his mother when he was first learning to walk. "I used to trip over my left foot a lot," Bryan laughingly recalls. "I was clumsy." Bryan's alter ego keeps challenges in perspective and chases pesky starlings away, so Bryan and wife Jennifer can focus on their new adventure of handcrafting world-class white wines.

Bryan's start in winemaking began in 1995 after he and Jennifer moved to the region. They became excited about the local wines, realizing northern Michigan's cool climate was similar to the climate of German wines he experienced while spending a semester of college in England. The wines produced in Germany's cool climate made a lasting impression. "I was exposed to a lot of wines when I lived in England, and I really liked the German wines," Bryan expresses.

It didn't take long before Bryan was hired as assistant winemaker at Peninsula Cellars, learning the trade under the tutelage of Lee Lutes, who moved on to become winemaker and a proprietor at Black Star Farms. Bryan took over as winemaker in 1998, earning proprietors Dave and Joan Kroupa dozens of wine awards during his 11-year career with them.

A humble winemaker, Bryan often credits his numerous awards to the quality climate and mature vineyards for producing great fruit. "What's fun are the wines—people getting excited about them," Bryan shares. "I love to get positive feedback for the region." Bryan also credits Jennifer as having an influence on the outcome of the wines as well.

It's possible that Bryan's diligence in crafting great wines stems from his theory that he has to drink what he makes.

"She helps me with the tastings," says Bryan about the winemaking process, "and she has a very good palate for dry whites."

A Gewürztraminer Bryan produced while working as Peninsula Cellars' winemaker has received much acclaim, earning numerous awards and high praise from syndicated wine writer Dan Berger and British wine author Tom Stevenson. Stevenson, author of *The Sotheby's Wine Encyclopedia, the Classic Reference to Wines Around the World*, states that Bryan "produced the first world-class Gewürztraminer outside of Alsace in 2002." Alsace is a world-renowned white wine region in France.

Bryan is fanatic about the whites as he believes varieties such as Riesling, Chardonnay, Pinot Gris, Pinot Blanc, and Gewürztraminer grow well naturally in the region's climate. "The reds are very good, but the whites are as good as anywhere in the world when grown here; Riesling in particular," Bryan claims.

To appease red wine drinkers, though, Bryan plans to offer one drier red wine, most likely a blend. "Reds are more inconsistent in the cool climate," explains Bryan. "When you have a good vintage, it's very good—remarkable."

It's possible that Bryan's diligence in crafting great wines stems from his theory that he has to drink what he makes. "I have to make good wine, because I have to drink it; it better taste good," Bryan chuckles.

When asked which wine he prefers, Bryan easily states, "I'm really into the Rieslings." Bryan, who plans to travel overseas frequently to meet with winemakers, is impressed with the wide selection of Rieslings available at most restaurants in Germany.

It's only fitting that Bryan's first release under the Left Foot Charley label is a Riesling. On the back of the label find Volume One of Left Foot Charley's journal where Bryan's alter ego agonizes over protecting his fruit against the crafty and quick starling and reflects on the vintage. Look for additional journal entries on future releases.

Bryan and Jennifer welcome customers to their new Traverse City tasting room in The Village at Grand Traverse Commons, home of the former state hospital abandoned nearly 20 years ago and the nation's largest historic preservation and adaptive reuse development project. The Ulbrich's urban facility includes 6,000 square feet of winemaking space for Bryan to experiment and further strengthen his position in the marketplace as a producer of world-class white wines. You can sample wines in the tasting room within the 100-year-old historic facility.

Bryan talks enthusiastically about his future in winemaking, as he shares, "I'm fired up." He plans to stay true to his white wine focus. "I'm passionate about whites because they grow so well in the area naturally," Bryan explains. "Having the ability to go with it rather than force it produces more exceptional wines."

GET IN TOUCH

806 Red Drive
Traverse City
(231) 995-0500
wine@leftfootcharley.com
www.leftfootcharley.com
GPS: N 44° 45.18282, W 085° 38.75976

Peninsula Cellars

A nineteenth-century schoolhouse is an enchanting respite along the traversing scenic drive amassed with vineyards, orchards, and multimillion dollar homes. The understated, former Maple Grove School is where the peninsula's children were educated from 1885 to 1955. Inside the one-room school building, you'll discover that a large rectangular tasting bar has replaced the classroom tables, yet Detention lives on as a red wine blend of all of Peninsula Cellars' last cut vineyards.

Proprietors Dave and Joan Kroupa are reminded daily of the myriad of Kroupas who attended the school as children "except for my grandfather," shares Dave. "He went to school on a boat on Bowers Harbor in the winter. I imagine it was because the captain could read, so he taught the children to read."

Fourth-generation farmer Dave oversees his family's more than 150-year-old, 250-acre farm that is mostly cherry orchards sprinkled with apple trees and, since 1991, grapevines. Dave and Joan opted to diversify their farm products after noting several new wineries opening for business in the northern Michigan region in the early 1990s. "The apple business just isn't the same," Dave confides. Experienced farmers, the Kroupas had very little winemaking knowledge. Thus, they brought in experienced winemakers to craft the family's wines.

Lee Lutes, now winemaker and a proprietor at Black Star Farms, helped the Kroupas get started with the winery's first vintages of Chardonnay and Riesling released in 1994. Lee trained Bryan Ulbrich, who, for

Fourth-generation farmer Dave oversees his family's more than 150-year-old, 250-acre farm that is mostly cherry orchards sprinkled with apple trees and, since 1991, grapevines.

nearly 12 years, won numerous awards for Peninsula Cellars' wines before venturing into his own winery business, Left Foot Charley, in spring 2007. We look forward to tasting wines by Peninsula Cellar's newest winemaker, who is sure to carry forth the tradition of crafting excellent wines.

Peninsula Cellars has built a reputation producing cool-climate white wines, although nearly 20 wines, including reds, dessert wines, and, of course, cherry and apple wines, are available for tasting. Cherries picked from the Kroupas' mature orchard are a hit in the White Cherry wine that is sweet, yet tart, while apples plucked from the Kroupas' trees make for a crisp, light wine full of apple flavors.

Since 1999, Peninsula Cellars' wines have been offered for tasting in the former Maple Grove School, whose charm reveals itself in the original school bell within the cupola atop the schoolhouse. Inside, the chalkboards highlight wines such as Old School Red, Old School White, and, of course, Detention. Perhaps it was in detention when "I will only drink good wine" was repeatedly written on one of the tasting room chalkboards—see it for yourself when you visit.

You're sure to get an education at the spacious wine bar, where you'll be invited to sample a vertical flight of Chardonnays from several vintages or one of their multiple award-winning wines. As Peninsula Cellars has received most recognition for their traditional, drier style whites, be sure to try the Gewürztraminer and Semidry Riesling, sure to surprise you for their drier styles. A winter favorite is the Riesling Ice Wine, with "intense honeysuckle aroma and tropical fruit flavors."

Another nod to history is newer customer favorite Hotrod Cherry, a wine that honors Michigan's automotive industry. The moniker was created after a loyal customer in the "hot rod" business shared that he enjoyed the wine and really liked the color and bottle, often giving the cherry wine as gifts to clients. This prompted the proprietors to replace the cherry tree on the bottle with red-hot flames and describe the wine as, "Check her out! She's got a sweet body. Under the hood, she packs a cherry big block with 750ml of road ready rumble! Mint condition!"

There's no need to raise your hand since questions are welcome. The winery team loves to educate and share information on the wines and winemaking process. And, if extra credit is what you're seeking, arrange a tour of their Pinot Grigio vineyard, adjacent to the tasting room.

Dave and Joan still consider themselves farmers rather than vintners, but have learned to enjoy the wine over the years. "I like the red wines," says Dave, a red meat-and-potato kind of guy, "and Joan likes the white wines."

GET IN TOUCH

11480 Center Road (M-37)
Traverse City
(231) 933-9787
coryn@peninsulacellars.com
www.peninsulacellars.com
GPS: N 44° 51.23688, W 085° 31.6776

Two Lads Winery

"We believe we have the best view on the peninsula," Two Lads proprietor Cornel Olivier proudly states. From atop the hill, "It seems as if you can drive a golf ball straight into East Bay." Together with partners Chris Baldyga and Dick Quartel, Chris' father-in-law, Cornel is producing distinctly dry red and sparkling wines.

Why Two Lads when there are three? Dick is more of a silent partner, whereas the two lads—rugby enthusiasts and long-time friends since Cornel relocated to Traverse City from South Africa—are the front men. You'll likely see Cornel, winemaker and vineyard manager, and Chris, sales and marketing chief, in the contemporary tasting room pouring their wines. Cornel allows the wine to come alive with its natural fruit flavors, rather than manipulate the fruit to be something it's not. "What the earth provides, the fruit produces," he believes.

Thirteen acres of Chardonnay, Pinot Gris, Cabernet Franc and Merlot grapevines give the partners their first vintage in 2007. Pinot Noir and additional Chardonnay vines are to be planted on the 58-acre vineyard vista overlooking Grand Traverse Bay.

GET IN TOUCH

16985 Smokey Hollow Road
Traverse City
(231) 223-7722
info@2LWinery.com
www.2Lwinery.com
GPS: N 44° 56.05176, W 085° 29.51718

Pioneer Wine Trail ❧

SOUTHEAST MICHIGAN

Over the years, the best vintners in the Old World discovered that the finest wines were produced from grapes grown on south-facing hillsides. These hillsides provided the best sun exposure for the entire growing season and cold air drainage for natural frost protection. They knew that grapes thrived in sandy, gravelly soil that allowed for good water drainage. Our region faces harsh winters, which means we must take extra precautions to protect our vines. When selecting vineyard land, we choose what fine winemakers have known for years— vineyard conditions with all the components needed to grow great grapes to produce world-class wines. The tops of our hills are warmer because cold air is heavier than warm air. This means that the old air drains downward, drawing warm air down over the hilltops, allowing our big reds to ripen fully, producing full-bodied wines.

The winemakers of our region proudly produce fine wines and invite you to compare them to any similarly priced fine wines from around the world.

— KIP BARBER, VINTNER,
LONE OAK VINEYARD ESTATE

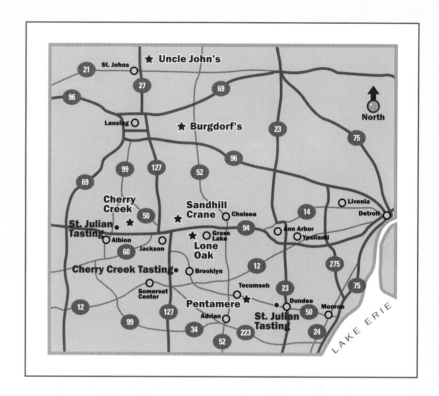

Burgdorf's Winery

Dave and Deb Burgdorf produced their first batch of wine more than 25 years ago in an attempt to salvage an abundant harvest of fresh, wild black raspberries. "We made several pies and cobblers and still had lots of raspberries left," Deb fondly recalls. Making wine seemed to be the next logical option for the couple with combined knowledge in agriculture and fermentation.

Dave and Deb have extensive knowledge of growing fruit and making wine, with Dave's degree in agriculture and 30 years experience in plants and conservation planning and Deb's degree in microbiology and over 15 years experience in fermentation. For a quarter of a century the Burgdorfs continued to make wine for friends and family, experimenting with several different fruits. "We experimented over the years on friends and got better and better," laughs Deb.

The raspberry wine was perfected over time. When they opened Burgdorf's Winery in 2005, the wine was naturally named Perfection. "Perfection, a black raspberry and tart cherry blend, is not the same as when it started. It evolved over the years," Deb shares as Dave chuckles. "We call it Perfection now, but it wasn't always so."

Sweet wine enthusiasts should also try the Winter Riesling, a great wine for sipping slowly. "On a scale of one to 10 on sweetness, the Winter Riesling is our 10," Dave describes. "It's a great dessert wine or a wine to take a little sip of before bed."

Dave and Deb make almost 20 small batches of wine, many of which are garnering regional attention. "We sent eight wines to the Indiana International Wine Competition during our first year just to get some feedback and won awards on six of them," Deb proudly boasts.

Most importantly, though, they encourage you to experience the wine your own way with no rights or wrongs. While Dave will take the time to show you how to sniff, taste, and enjoy, he will not tell you what you should expect as your own experience is likely to be different than anyone else's.

A fun way to experience the essence of winemaking is to make a batch of your own. Dave and Deb work alongside you, sharing winemaking knowledge and equipment while you make your own creation from a selection of 30 varieties. Take home your bottled wine with your own personalized label—an experience they say, "You'll remember for a lifetime."

The myriad of clocks in the tasting room are a reminder that each wine experience is about the time you are sharing. "Wine is a great icebreaker. After a little wine, you're all having fun. It's not only about the wine. The wine provides the avenue to get together, enjoy each other, and to have a good time. It's all about a 'moment' in wine," Dave feels.

Make the time to linger on the patio out back, which can also be reserved for private wine tastings and dinner parties. An old, odd-looking grill is sure to catch your eye, as we found it amusing and practical at the same time. "I made the grill from an old keg in college," Dave laughs, "and we're still using it today."

GET IN TOUCH

5635 Shoeman Road
Haslett
(517) 655-2883
wine@burgdorfwinery.com
www.burgdorfwinery.com
GPS: N 42° 44.88174, W 084° 20.868

Cherry Creek Cellars

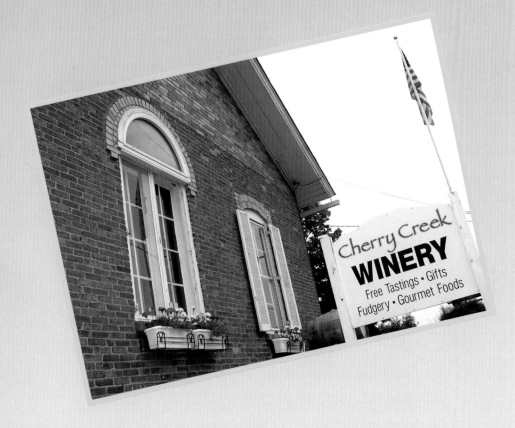

Fifty-two inland lakes dot the hilly Irish Hills region near Jackson and surround a restored 1870 schoolhouse, where you can taste wines crafted by John Burtka of Cherry Creek Cellars. Be sure to grab and pull the schoolhouse bell rope to loudly announce your visit.

Children who accompany parents to the winery, fudgery, and gift shop are invited to do the rope-pulling honors before adults are served. "The effort needed to clang the bell often surprises our young visitors," laughs John.

The Old Schoolhouse, as the Burtkas have affectionately named their tasting room, may seem to be in an obscure location, albeit winery traffic is surpassing the steady flow of visitors at their vineyard and tasting room in Parma, just west of Jackson. John attributes the newer tasting room's success to the schoolhouse charm as well as to his wife Denise, who is a great hostess.

"We're also minutes from M-50 and M-52 and just three minutes from Michigan Speedway," shares Denise. The Irish Hills region is a popular and affordable vacation area for those residing in southern Michigan, due to its enormous number of lakes and access to golf courses and family-friendly miniature golf courses, as well as to one of Michigan's oldest state parks, W. J. Hayes.

The original brick exterior topped by a whitewashed bell tower stands out along antique valley on U.S. 12. The original 1870 architectural inscription is a testament to the generations of learning that have occurred within the small schoolhouse walls. If your visit coincides with running into the winery's owners, John or Denise, or good friend Al Herman, you're sure to learn a thing or two about making—and appreciating—Michigan wine.

"Yes, there's a technique to enjoying a good glass of wine," John enthuses. "The most important thing, though? Simply enjoying it; if you like it, drink it."

Cherry Creek Cellars first opened in 2003. John hit the ground running by hosting delectable gourmet dinners, prepared by Chef Marian Gray and paired with his handcrafted wines. We were among the first to try out his wine pairing dinners and were notably impressed with John's charisma and talent at putting everyone at ease.

"Wine is to be enjoyed, whether it's swirled, sniffed, and gurgled first, or simply savored to ease the strain of a busy day." John often initiates humor to encourage guests to check their inhibitions at the door.

John's passion for winemaking was instilled in him by his late father, John Burtka Sr., who was a hobby winemaker throughout John's youth. The son gives much of the credit for the opening of Cherry Creek Cellars to his father with whom he shared a close bond until his passing in 2005.

One of John's most memorable lessons was making red wine in his basement in a big tub when the family's enthusiasm got a bit out of hand, flooding the red juice onto the white-carpeted floor. "It was a

painful, yet well-learned, lesson," laughs John. "We now make wine far away from white walls and carpets."

The days of winemaking in his basement are far behind. At Cherry Creek Cellars' busy Parma winery and vineyard, you can see John's Pinot Noir grapevines gracing the hillside. Expect an intimate experience at the tasting bar where wines are artfully poured. Sharp, jazzy wine labels, designed by Michigan artists, wrap Jazz, a sweet red wine with raspberry flavors, and John's oh-so-delicious Black Raspberry dessert wine, Fetter Hahn. The Fetter Hahn is a favorite of ours for dinner parties and holiday meals.

"Customers who love our big, bold reds love our Fetter Hahn."

"Customers who love our big, bold reds love our Fetter Hahn," shares John. "Pour the port-like wine into small chocolate cups and then savor the chocolate soaked with black raspberry tones."

And big, bold reds he has. Enigma, an incredible Cabernet Sauvignon with cherry and black currant blended with the dark grape, boasts mysterious undertones. Cabernet Franc is very smooth with hints of plum and cedar and a long finish. This customer favorite often showcases Collector Series artwork, as well as original artwork by Michigan artist Kim Fujiwara.

Notably, the winery earned seven medals at the 2006 Michigan Wine and Spirits Competition, including Double Gold and two additional golds. Cherry Creek also earned several medals, including gold and silvers, at the international American Wine Society's annual commercial wine competitions.

Within the walls of the Old Schoolhouse, you'll discover a gleaming, knotty-pine bar built from a wall added to the schoolhouse when a previous owner converted it to a hunting cabin. The wall was torn down by the Burtkas to reclaim the original open space. Two small bedrooms used to fill the space where the tasting bar stands today. A charming legacy left by the cabin owner is a set of delicately brushed-on, hand-painted tiles on the bathroom walls, reflecting the schoolhouse in seasons.

Original maple flooring, patched with newer pine and maple planks, adds character to the expansive interior. A clear glass case cleverly displays Denise's freshly made, two-inch-thick square fudge, while wood racks stack gourmet jellies and spreads made in the Irish Hills region.

We assure you, you won't leave Cherry Creek Cellars empty-handed. Packing wine, cookie-topped white-chocolate fudge, and Heavenly Hash chocolate fudge with our Vintner's Blend coffee, we shuffle to our cars, feeling completely satisfied.

GET IN TOUCH

2199 North Concord Road
Albion
(517) 531-3080
inquire@cherrycreekwine.com
www.cherrycreekwine.com
GPS: N 42° 15.85182, W 084° 38.93484

Tasting Room:
15750 U.S. 12
Cement City
(517) 592-4663
GPS: N 42° 3.02826, W 084° 18.10476

Lone Oak Vineyard Estate

The pioneer who kick-started the Pioneer Wine Trail in southeast Michigan is a confident risk taker obsessed with growing grapes. Kip Barber, along with wife Dennise, was the first to boldly pronounce the area perfect for vines, planting more than 12 German and French grape varietals on 25 acres of prime land, located along I-94 between Ann Arbor and Jackson.

Kip found his ideal hillside after nine months of scouring topographical maps, driving hundreds of miles, and knocking on doors to inquire if land was for sale. "I was determined to grow my own vineyard on south-facing hills with easy highway access," Kip recalls. "After months of heartache and disappointment, I found these hills."

Kip tore away overgrown branches on a "For Sale by Owner" sign. Like other properties before, he knocked on a door—only this time, the land owner said that the property was, indeed, for sale.

The former woodworker became a confident farmer and vintner after testing his theories in a small backyard covered with vines in Ferndale. With the help of a how-to book on making wine, Kip and Dennise turned their backyard hobby into a full-time business and passion once they found their dream property.

They deemed the acreage in Jackson ideal for growing grapes. Kip claims the sandy, gravelly loam soil is consistent with France's Bordeaux region. And although the temperature is milder in that region, Kip believes their land is ideal for growing healthy

"The best way to grow grapes in Michigan's cold climate is low to the ground."

European varietals. They opened Lone Oak Vineyard Estate in 2002, naming their winery for the lone oak tree with deep roots in the midst of the vineyard.

"We cleared the land, but just couldn't part with the oak tree," says Dennise. "Together, we can't even get our arms around it." So the tree stayed. Other trees removed when they planted their vines have been salvaged for use in their future timber-frame dream home, to be custom crafted by Kip, who will apply skills finessed over nearly 25 years of woodworking.

You'll certainly notice the atypical, low-growing vines when you pull into their drive. "The best way to grow grapes in Michigan's cold climate is low to the ground," Kip firmly believes and practices. His

distinctive growing system is an indication of the precise efforts that go into the bold flavored wines produced at Lone Oak Vineyard Estate.

He first planted vines in 1997 to create a canopy that benefits from the earth's natural heat, ensuring the vines are never exposed to temperatures 10 degrees below zero. In winter, Kip covers the vines with wood chips to keep them insolated.

"Freezing cold temperatures cause damage to many wine varieties," Kip likes to educate. "My approach to growing grapes low to the ground is fail-proof because of the natural vine covering." He claims he's the only vintner in Michigan to grow Zinfandel, a grape that is difficult to winterize. "I essentially bury the vines in the winter," Kip insights. "I can grow Zinfandel because of my system."

Another sight you'll typically see is the Barbers' wine dogs, Ozzy and Mabel, who will boisterously greet you. In the modest tasting room, you'll be invited to taste a selection of white, red, and dessert wines, including their popular Fleur Blanche, which translates to white flower in French. The Seyval Blanc–Vignoles blend is a sweet white wine that is presented in an elegant, blue bottle.

Red wine drinkers can enjoy the estate-grown Vin due Roi, Wine of the King, a Bordeaux-style blend of Cabernet Sauvignon, Cabernet Franc, Merlot, and Petite Verdot. A favorite of ours is the softer Pioneer Red, a blend of red grapes with hints of black cherry and plum. Other customer favorites include the Merlot and Riesling. "Our customers say they love our big Merlot—they can't believe it's a Michigan wine," shares Dennise.

The Barbers' newer vines include Petite Sirah and Sauvignon Blanc, giving the pioneers plenty of estate-grown grapes with which to handcraft wines. Future plans include building a hilltop home with a southern view of the Irish Hills region and Goose Lake, and a northern view overlooking a new tasting room, restaurant, outdoor amphitheater, and, of course, their lone oak tree.

In the meantime, Kip and Dennise wish to expand their tasting room to include a 60-seat venue where light sandwiches and cheese platters are served, euchre tournaments and checker challenges are frequent, and musical entertainment provides the background to great conversations.

"We want this to be a place where our customers can unwind in a smoke-free environment on a Friday or Saturday night," invites Dennise. "We truly have a big vision for what this can be."

GET IN TOUCH

8400 Ann Arbor Road
Grass Lake
(517) 522-8167
kip@loneoakvineyards.com
www.loneoakvineyards.com
GPS: N 42° 17.28042, W 084° 15.84702

Pentamere Winery

Behind a revived 1880s storefront in Tecumseh's bustling downtown district is a group of good-hearted friends who came together to bring you great wine.

On any given day, you'll be greeted by one of Pentamere's proprietors, husband and wife team, Dan and Maria Measel, who instigated the opening of the winery; brothers Nathan and Peter Sparks, who lend hands in chemistry and as jacks of all trades; and Ed and Annie Gerten, who manage day-to-day operations and whip up delicious fare for busy workdays, respectively.

Feel comfortable and right at home tasting wines traditional to Michigan, such as Chardonnay and a well-balanced Cherry Wine the winery owners claim is the "best cherry wine in Michigan." We encourage you to try the more unusual wines to the region, such as Zweigelt, a full-bodied, spicy red varietal from Austria. Chambourcin, Pentamere's self-titled "Great Lakes Chianti" offers hints of cedar and strawberry and a light acid finish for those who enjoy a nice drier red wine.

Ed also doesn't want you to miss tasting their award-winning Gewürztraminer, a classic, dry white wine that won a silver medal at the 2006 Great Lakes Wine Competition. Their 2004 Eiswein, German for ice wine, nabbed gold at the Great Lakes Wine Competition.

Regardless of whether you enjoy your wine sweet or very, very dry, your taste buds rule here. Maria encourages you to "drink what tastes good to you" and while the team takes their wine very seriously, they don't take themselves too seriously at all. Their sense of humor and ability to have fun shine through all aspects of the winery. Dan's theory is "a bad day at the winery is better than a good day at the office."

Their humor is most evident in their creative, informal titles; Dan's CFO title, for Chief Fermenting Officer; Ed's title of Chief Schmoozing Officer; and Peter's LAG title, standing for "Long-Arm Galoot" useful for brick repair and computer trouble-shooting. Our personal favorite, though, is Maria's title, "She Who Must Be Obeyed."

This jovial team of winery owners is passionate for making your visit to their winery a pleasant and comfortable one. "Each month we feature an artist from the region," shares Ed, whose more official title is business manager. "We enjoy giving new artists a starting point for showcasing their work."

Artwork is hung on the red-hued brick wall that was uncovered during 14 months of renovation. "It was a little shop of horrors," Dan shakes his head recalling. "We stuck to the linoleum floor; there were low-dropped ceilings; and greasy chili-pepper wallpaper covered the walls." The nineteenth-century space was revived into an urban winery with historic appeal after the partners ripped up the old linoleum, tore down the chili pepper décor, and pulled out an estimated 324,623 nails from molding and framing—and, yes, they did the labor and the math.

Perhaps the most noticeable feature of the winery, though, is the open flooring that allows you to overlook the winemaking in the basement cellar. Prior to cutting out the substantial, rectangular opening, the owners accessed the cellar by treading lightly down a narrow staircase that required a turn halfway down to avoid a beam overhead.

Dan shares that he "chalked a line, took a circular saw and zipped through the old flooring" to create the wide open space in which to view the wine making and, from Dan's perspective, "get the steel tanks in." It's a little known fact that they had to "valet park their tanks" in order to work with them, the group enjoys joking. Also down below are 10 American oak and two French oak barrels used for ageing the winery's Cabernet Sauvignon, Chambourcin, Merlot, and Chardonnay.

It's fascinating to look down on the winemaker as he's atop his ladder, stirring up two tons of Chambourcin just in from Ohio in a huge stainless steel tank imported from Italy. Grapes arrive from all over the Great Lakes basin, from the western shores of Michigan to Ontario's Niagara Peninsula; hence, the name Pentamere, which is loosely translated from Latin and Old English and combined to mean "five lakes."

When we asked Dan if what you see at the winery was his vision from the beginning, he quickly replied, "Er, no. It evolved during the course of the renovation." What also evolved was Dan's interest in winemaking, which he claims was a "rolling obsession."

This jovial team of winery owners is passionate for making your visit to their winery a pleasant and comfortable one.

When you visit, Ed encourages you to "ask questions, learn about our wine, and meet some friendly people."

"My buddy, Sam Goodin, was making wine. I helped him out and the wine tasted pretty darn good," Dan fondly recalls. "We said 'we can do this.' Right then, it was like the heavens opened up and, all of a sudden, I had permission to do this." Dan laughs that in his characteristic way, it became an obsession. He did a lot of reading, went to trade shows, made more wine, and proclaimed, "This is doable."

Dan and Maria began looking for property to plant a vineyard, with their good friends Sam and his wife Donna encouraging them all the way. They didn't have any luck finding an ideal piece of land within their price point. The abandoned Mexican restaurant with its spacious windows overlooking Tecumseh's main thoroughfare offered the Measels the visibility they were seeking for promoting and selling their wines. Nathan and Peter were on board from the beginning with the winery and Ed and Annie quickly joined the team as proprietors as well.

Pentamere's proprietors are happy to give tours of their stoned-in cellar during your visit and share their photo album showcasing the "gruesome before photos" of this now lovely, historically preserved experience.

When you visit, Ed encourages you to "ask questions, learn about our wine, and meet some friendly people." Dan adds that, "You should have the same comfort level coming into our winery as going into a coffee shop or into Mike's burger place down the street. Wine is food; it's a part of life."

Maria is excited about their Harvest Apple, describing it as "lip-smacking and tangy," created from Fuji-like tasting apples from Kapnick Orchard down the road. The same apples are used to create Mystic Apple with a splash of cranberry to give it a refreshing, fall flavor ideal for hearty meals of roasted turkey and ham.

Wine jellies, made with Cabernet Franc and Chardonnay grapes, are prepared by Pentamere's team in their local church's large, industrial kitchen. "It's wonderful on a hot croissant, bagel, or muffin," Ed touts.

Go to Pentamere Winery for great wine and food, and you're sure to laugh and learn a thing or two about the grapes and winemaking process. Taste handcrafted wines produced below street level and we're sure you'll leave smiling.

GET IN TOUCH

131 East Chicago Boulevard (M-50)
Tecumseh
(517) 423-9000
dan@pentamerewinery.com
www.pentamerwinery.com
GPS: N 42° 0.25422, W 083° 56.6796

Sandhill Crane Vineyards

The sandhill cranes' height and distinct strut and call make these birds a favorite among bird watchers. Named for these regal birds that gather in the surrounding area and are often seen during our visits, Sandhill Crane Vineyards' surprisingly secluded setting off busy I-94 fulfills the vision of the Moffatt family.

Norman Moffatt, the family patriarch, was a hobby winemaker for 40 years before he began commercially producing wines. When we asked Norm why he began winemaking many years ago, the retired Detroit police officer matter-of-factly replies, "I've always wanted to make wine, so I made it."

Norm's wife Alice is a familiar face in the winery, as is his sister, Anne Leisinger, and two daughters, Heather Price and Holly Balansag, who learned winemaking as her father's apprentice. Wine dog Rosé, an Airedale terrier, is also a frequent greeter, reaching many a waist with the top of her head.

Heather, the winery's director, shares, "The original plan was for Dad to have more time to putter with the grapes, and Mom and Aunt Anne to spend weekends working the tasting room counter."

The Moffat family never looked back when customer demand immediately launched the winery into a busy operation. "Our customers have responded to our wines from the beginning," states Heather. "We've also listened to what our customers have to say about our wines and have evolved to meet the demand."

Alice and Rosé stroll along the vineyard.

Today, Holly is official winemaker whose passion and natural talent is evident in her "odd, quirky blends" that have become customer favorites. She can't keep her award-winning Rhapsody in Red, a sweet red wine with a splash of raspberry, on the winery's shelves, as new vintages quickly sell out.

During an early fall visit, Holly was in the throes of pressing 1,000 pounds of fresh raspberries from a local farmer for her 100 percent raspberry dessert wine. This time, the job was much easier with a new steel automated press. What used to take hours and sometimes days with a hand press now takes much less time. "My arms used to get so tired moving the crank up and down to press the fruit," Holly recalls. "I save a ton of energy and time with the new press."

For summertime sipping, Heather recommends Vidal Blanc, which she describes as "a fruity wine with apple on the nose, peach on the finish, and subtle hints of pear, apricot, and sweet grass." This is one of our favorite warm-weather wines to enjoy on the deck or beachside watching the sunset. Another popular white wine is their dry Traminette, a honey-floral wine with a hint of melon.

We also like the winery's Proprietor's Reserve Chancellor, a velvety red with hints of plum and blackberry. As an "unfiltered and really nice red," Heather shares that it "cellars very well." For red wine enthusiasts, the winery also produces a traditional Merlot and Moulin Rouge, a dry red Bordeaux-style blend of Cabernet Sauvignon, Cabernet Franc, and Chancellor.

Newer to winery operations is the production of ports, with Holly producing "really yummy" Blueberry and Blackberry port wines. "Whatever you enjoy drinking; go for it," Heather encourages. "We have no rules. If you enjoy a wine, drink it."

Don't miss the winery's annually sponsored Sandhill Crane Festival in October that combines watching thousands of cranes flock to a nearby sanctuary, followed by wine tasting and hot, mulled wine.

GET IN TOUCH

4724 Walz Road
Jackson
(517) 764-0679
info@sandhillcranevineyards.com
www.sandhillcranevineyards.com
GPS: N 42° 18.08898, W 084° 17.6811

Seasonal Tasting Room:
Dexter Cider Mill
3685 Central Street
(734) 426-8101
GPS: N 42° 20.45028, W 083° 52.80462

Uncle John's Fruit House Winery

Five generations of apple farming is a long time to get creative with diversifying your family's primary agricultural product. Uncle John's has spun its apple line from raw apples and cider to caramel apples, pies, and breads. Topping off the offerings are the more recent additions of apple wine, hard apple cider, and apple brandy.

The centennial Beck farm was first established by Frank Beck more than 12 decades ago when its orchards produced apples and its fields grew raspberries and strawberries. The Beck apples were a popular product in the 1970s when fourth-generation John and Carolyn Beck sold them by the bushel off their front door step. It wasn't until 1972, after receiving several requests by frequent visitors to make cider, that Uncle John's Cider Mill was established. An early 1900s cattle barn, located on the farm and formerly used by the Beck family to raise cows, sheep, and horses, hosted the new mill.

Today, Uncle John's produces 55,000 gallons of homemade cider each year during apple harvest time in September and October. Production of the apple cider can be viewed from an overlook, where you can enjoy fresh apple cider and donuts while watching handpicked apples make their way through the large mill to be sanitized and cleaned before being chopped and pressed into cider.

After taking a wagon ride and finding our way through the corn maze, we warmed up with hot cider and pumpkin donuts in the mill. We took home a peck (a quarter bushel) of Honey Crisp

"My family has been making hard cider for years and years; my father, my grandfather, and way before that."

produced on the farm, and considered premium eating apples. They were absolutely delicious and crunchy with both sweet and tart flavors. In addition to the multitude of apple varieties, Uncle John's produce line has also expanded into asparagus, blueberries, cherries, corn, peaches, pumpkins, squash, and gourds.

The latest endeavor of the 120-year-old, five-generation-run fruit farm is Uncle John's Fruit House Winery, located in a 1918 former fruit barn located on the property. With fresh fruit production integral to his family's heritage, winemaker and fifth-generation Mike Beck, Uncle John's son, has produced more than 20 fruit-blended wines featuring hints of cherry, peach, apple, pear, raspberry, and blueberry, in addition to traditional grape blends.

The charming yet chic tasting room, where you must try house favorite Harvest Apple, is a destination or quick break from the myriad of activities at Uncle John's. Also be sure to sample Mike's favorite, Gewürztraminer. "I enjoy making the Gewürz because I enjoy drinking Gewürz," Mike smiles.

While tasting, don't miss Mike's string of hard ciders, called Farmhouse Ciders, with flavors of apple, pear, and other seasonal varieties. Producing hard cider was a natural transition for the family business as Mike shares, "My family has been making hard cider for years and years; my father, my grandfather, and way before that."

Mike explains that making cider commercially is a little different than making cider for friends and family, "Because of regulations, you can't put in some of the really good stuff like raisins and corn that bring out even more flavors." After sampling some of Mike's tasty hard apple cider, it's impossible not to enjoy its full, natural flavor.

To produce the latest Beck product, apple spirits, Mike imported a copper and brass still from Germany. "It's a German pot-still designed for brandy production meant to bring out all of the fruit characteristics," explains Mike. The brandy is then aged in oak Bourbon barrels from Kentucky for about four years before it's released. "The inside is charred rather than toasted like most oak barrels," Mike describes. "The char brings out more unique flavors."

On top of great products, Uncle John's offers a wide variety of fun activities for the whole family. Take train and wagon rides through the orchards, test your luck in the corn and bale mazes during pumpkin-picking time, take a stroll through the gift shops, or take a hike down a nature trail. You can also join in on the fun during one of their events scheduled throughout the year. End your experience by warming up with hot cider and fresh donuts in the mill or grabbing snacks in the deli and bakery.

Uncle John's is truly a destination for the whole family to spend the day for a fun adventure.

Keep your eye out for Uncle John, who is often seen in his jean overalls around the farm. While Mike is the one who now runs the daily operations, his dad is never too far away, ready to jump in where help is needed. In fact, it was Uncle John himself driving the tractor of our wagon ride back to the mill as the regular driver needed to leave early. Uncle John's is truly a destination for the whole family to spend the day for a fun adventure.

GET IN TOUCH

8614 North U.S. 127
St. Johns
(989) 224-3686
cider@ujcidermill.com
www.fruithousewinery.com
GPS: N 43° 6.73668, W 084° 33.77466

Hard Cider: Making Its Way into Michigan's Wineries

At many stops along the wine trails, you'll discover a new offering: hard cider. Hard cider, typically crafted from apples, is produced by pressing juice from the fruit which is then fermented, resulting in a refreshing, low-alcohol beverage. Apple tends to be the flavor of choice while other varieties in Michigan include Perry, made from the juice of pears, Cyser, when honey is added to the apple juice, and Apple Cherry, a blend of apples and cherries. Like most hard ciders, the Michigan varieties tend to be sweet in flavor. Be sure to ask for a taste when visiting one of the wineries that is helping to lead the charge in Michigan's hard cider movement.

Beyond the Trails

Like all endeavors of the heart, starting a
winery outside well-established viticulture regions
requires an initial romantic spark, followed up
with truckloads of grapes and boatloads of vigor.

These small wineries, although off the beaten
trail, offer something unique to wine enthusiasts.
Without the confines of a single vineyard, these
wineries benefit by their ability to purchase
grapes from many different regions of the state,
including citrusy Chardonnays and garnet red
Cabernets from the southwest region, flinty
Rieslings and fruity Gewürztraminers from
the northwest region, and fruity hybrids from
both regions.

Each one of these winemakers produces distinctly
different blends of wines, each with their own
methods and practices, and each with their own
style—contributing to their ability to produce
some very unique and exquisite wines. Regardless
of style, you should expect to find a Michigan
wine when in Michigan. Like Germany,
Michigan's climate produces cooler-climate wines.
When our climate is matched with the proper
variety of grapes, we can produce some of
the world's finest wines.

— RALPH STABILE, VINTNER,
MACKINAW TRAIL WINERY

Jomagrha Vineyards and Winery

Travel halfway up or halfway down Michigan's west coast in the Lower Peninsula to find the charming summer resort community of Pentwater. A few miles north of the beach town in the lush green hills of the Pere Marquette State Forest and over the county line is Jomagrha Vineyards and Winery. The winery is a five-minute drive off the highway and around a bend in the silhouette of the Three Sisters, a vista that unfurls atop three distinct hills that overlook the region.

An early last-century, white-painted wood barn bearing the weight of a 300-pound grapevine wreath juts above the quaint vineyard. Beat up trucks strategically placed among the vines are moved nightly to give the impression that there are workers on the farm. Combined with the low-tech tactic of airing music through speakers into the vineyard, the trucks provide the winemaker with some level of defense against his biggest crop threat—deer.

A mostly one-man show, Jomagrha's winemaker and proprietor John Sanford produces an impressive selection of limited-quantity table wines, many of which are named for the area. Three Sisters is a light blush wine made with Vignoles grapes, while Bison Red is a hearty De Chaunac and Chancellor blend. The Bison Red gets its name from the previous owner's flower stand enterprise. To attract customers, he kept bison on his property. "My grapevines flourish due to the nutrients in the soil," John smiles.

John hand cares for his seven acres of vines, crushes grapes, and crafts and bottles his wines for retail sales in his modest tasting room within the vineyard.

Son Harry has lent a hand in production in the past and help is a town away in friends Dave Wilson and Mark Babinec, who helped John clear the land for this vineyard in 1998.

"Thanks to Mark, my Bison Red won a Silver Medal at the Michigan State Fair," shares John. "I had to step away from one of our winemaking batches and Mark, helping out, inadvertently added some Chancellor grapes to what was going to be simply De Chaunac." Today, the wine continues to be a best seller.

Other visitor favorites are named for Jomagrha's proximity to Lake Michigan. October Sunset is a blend of apple and raspberry; its color reflects the clear evening glow of a Lake Michigan sunset. John shares that many customers buy this wine just for its name; we bought it for the name and the taste. We really enjoy his Maréchal Foch, and his Pinot Gris is a great crisp, white wine.

John's passion for winemaking sprouted after an eighth-grade science project on fermentation. After a few careers, including 13 years as a hydrographic surveyor for land and marine projects in the oil and petroleum industry, John has found his calling in producing wines as a full-time venture.

John's farming ethic was established working on his grandparents' farms throughout high school. It was this early experience that solidified his love of the outdoors and for experimenting with anything he planted. "I have always had a picture of a family farm in the back of my mind throughout my career," says John. As John's wife Mary grew up in nearby Hart and John's hometown of Shelby was the school rival, they settled on Pentwater as a compromise within arm's reach of their hometowns.

John planted 23 grape varieties in a test lot to see which were best suited for the farm, a mile east of Lake Michigan. He began producing wine for family use and it quickly grew beyond his available space. "The laundry room was filled up with jugs," John laughingly recalls. "After dropping a seven-gallon carboy of red wine in the laundry area, I had to move my winery operations."

He started Jomagrha Vineyards and Winery in 1999, building the winery and tasting room himself. He handcrafted the cherrywood tasting bar from lumber his father saved from trees harvested from a relative's farm in the 1960s. Naming his winemaking venture

159

was easy. "Jomagrha consists of the first two letters of each of my family members: John, Mary, and sons Graham and Harry," shares John.

The winery's first bottled wine is their most popular white, Old Lady White, which John admits isn't always responded to warmly due to the name. When the wine was bottled, they struggled with finding the right name. John and Mary decided to quickly, and humorously, label the wine "Old Lady White" as a surprise for a friend who was turning 50. She loved the wine—and the name—and insisted the wine maintain its moniker, while another frequent customer prefers to add a "G" in front of "Old" with a black marker.

John is a very down-to-earth vintner who enjoys taking the time to pour his own wines. When you visit with him, you may note the antique grand piano against the wall. The solid mahogany 1856 piano traveled by train to Chicago before being carried by horse and buggy to nearby Benona Township and the Parson family. The piano remained in the Parson family and, eventually, ended up in a pole barn until John placed an ad in the paper seeking a piano for his son Graham. The Parson family invited the Sanfords to their house to consider their piano. "Mrs. Parson told my son, 'young man, if you promise to play it, you can have it,'" John divulges. "At the time, we didn't know the piano was worth anything." The cast-iron harp and handwritten "tuned and repaired in 1877" and "tuned and repaired in 1879" within the piano further bear the piano's provenance and awe John and us with its history.

Today, Graham continues to pursue a career as a pianist as well as a fashion designer. As Mary prefers her electric piano and John spends up to 100 hours a week in the vineyard, with no time to pursue his musical passions, the stately old grand piano sits mostly idle in his tasting room. Time your visit for the holiday season and you may catch Graham in town playing classics and his favorite melodies for seasonal entertainment.

Overlooking the stately antique is another reminder of John's career path to hitting his stride as a wine-maker. A framed commendation from NASA hangs as the focal point amid a world map wallpapered on one of the tasting room's walls. The honor recognizes John's role in assisting with the space shuttle Challenger recovery in 1986.

John's career came full circle a few years ago. His eighth-grade science teacher visited the winery for John's expert advice on growing and pruning grapes.

GET IN TOUCH

7365 South Pere Marquette Highway
Pentwater
(231) 869-4236
john@jomagrha.com
www.jomagrha.com
GPS: N 43° 49.40712, W 086° 23.92206

Krolczyk Cellars

Rainy Days and Cool Nights are two of the first releases from Krolczyk Cellars, along with Cabernet Franc, a dry red with intense flavors and a bold finish. Dan Krolczyk, who believes "there's nothing more engaging than producing wine," started making great beverages as an assistant brewer at Kuhnhenn's in Warren before venturing to L. Mawby Vineyards to learn the art of winemaking. Dan is currently crafting small batches of wine, available in a few retail stores around the state or by phone. Dan plans to expand the business with six new releases in 2007 including Cabernet Franc, Maréchal Foch, Riesling, Chardonnay, and a couple of blends and hopes to have a tasting room someday.

GET IN TOUCH

(586) 764-7709
joni@kcellars.com
www.kcellars.com

Mackinaw Trail Winery

Twenty-five miles by boat across Lake Michigan from Door County, Wisconsin, and less than two hours west by car after crossing the Mackinac Bridge is Mackinaw Trail Winery. Situated along the Manistique River within a dune stroll out to the 1915 Manistique East Breakwater Lighthouse, it's a destination worth reaching.

Handcrafted wines produced from grapes grown in the southwest corner of our state and, in the near future, in the Upper Peninsula, are creating a buzz in the wine industry. "Wine in the U.P.?" You bet.

The wines are produced by vintner Raffael "Ralph" Stabile, who developed a passion for winemaking and for learning his ancestral trade from his Sicilian grandparents. "My grandfather's brother brought vines over from Italy, which they planted in Mt. Clemens. The one-acre plot kept producing sour grapes. I don't think they had the right grapes for the climate," Ralph laughingly recalls.

His grandparents kept making wine in "big barrels" in their basement, though. Their zest for winemaking had a lasting impact on Ralph, while his other siblings had no interest. "I'm the only one in the whole family who loves making wine," shares Ralph.

Ralph's family relocated to the Upper Peninsula from downtown Detroit when he was 15. "It was a culture shock," Ralph reminisces. Ralph graduated from Newberry High School and later met Laurie, a native of Naubinway. It was after a stint in the military, followed by a career as a Technology Engineer in Green Bay, Wisconsin, that Ralph pursued his dream to become a vintner.

Ralph and Laurie established their Mackinaw Trail Winery tasting room in Manistique in 2005 to be convenient to travelers arriving by water or roadway. The tasting room is located next to the marina along the Manistique River and on the shores of the Lake Michigan harbor, where you can dock your boat while wine tasting. You'll love watching the boats sail by over a crisp glass of Harbor Light White.

Ralph's big seller is Big Red, a favorite campfire wine that is a full bodied and semidry. We're told it's already an Upper Peninsula favorite. Ralph also recommends taking his crisp North Shore White, crafted from Vignoles, to barbeques—touting that it complements any meat on the grill. "It's our best-selling wine," he says. It earned a silver medal at its first competition.

The wine list also includes Cabernet Franc aged in French oak, which took home gold at its first entrance in the annual Michigan Wine and Spirits Competition. Unlike the Cabernet Franc, their Cabernet Sauvignon is aged in Minnesota oak resulting in two distinct big reds crafted by Ralph.

Ralph produces both un-oaked and oaked Chardonnay, while the Blueberry Melange, released each fall, is a creamy surprise. "We're making a Riesling as well," says Ralph, who gets his vinifera grapes from Michigan's southwest region, as they don't grow well in temperatures below 10 degrees.

Great Lakes seafood lovers will be delighted to find smoked fish and fresh salmon, trout, whitefish, walleye, and, in season, chubs arriving daily from King Fishery in Naubinway, operated by Laurie's dad. The tasting room used to be the old fishery until Laurie's family relocated it. "The fish used to drop right onto the floor," explains Ralph. "Now the water is too low to bring the fish in."

Another extension of Ralph and Laurie's winemaking business is the bold planting of cold-hardy hybrid

"They'll survive more than one frost," Ralph assuredly states. "The Garden Peninsula's climate is only two days off Leelanau Peninsula and Old Mission Peninsula climates. We share similar growing conditions, although we get more snow and more frosts. When the snow covers the vines, it's good for them." Wines produced from these grapes are a few years out; however, we're eager to try these northern-grown wines. Look for Fayette Estate Vineyards as the Stabiles' second label when the first vintage is released.

The destination Ralph and Laurie have created for you is worth reaching. This land, if you've never visited, is truly God's country, with miles of dunes, breathtaking cliffs, deep harbors, and unspoiled beauty … and, making it even better, Michigan wine.

grapes on Garden Peninsula, about 17 miles south of Manistique. They plan to acquire acreage near Fayette Historic State Park to plant a vineyard with grapes that have proven themselves in 30-below temperatures.

Ralph's vines will consist of Frontenac Gris, St. Croix, La Crescent, La Crosse, and St. Pepin. These hybrids may not be familiar sounding yet; Ralph says they've been tested in Minnesota and Wisconsin's coldest climates. He's also considering planting some New York varieties as well.

GET IN TOUCH

103 West Lakeshore Drive
Manistique
(906) 341-2303
stabile@mackinawtrailwinery.com
www.mackinawtrailwinery.com
GPS: N45° 57.21756, W 086° 14.93718

Experience the Upper Peninsula

Mackinaw Trail Winery gives you the perfect excuse to take that long-overdue trip to Michigan's Upper Peninsula, a naturalist's paradise. After crossing the Mackinac Bridge to St. Ignace, take U.S. 2 and a quick left to the Bridge View Park overlook for an unparalleled view of Mackinac Bridge and the Lower Peninsula.

Hop back on U.S. 2 and make a quick right to fill up at Clyde's, an old-fashion drive-in restaurant famous for giant double-decker burgers. If the kids are along for the ride, hit the Mystery Spot, a childhood favorite for its mysterious gravity-defying illusions.

West along U.S. 2 to Mackinaw Trail Winery in Manistique, travel through several miles of dunes that offer the perfect excuse for picnicking and catching an evening sunset.

Dip down into Garden Peninsula, about 17 miles on Delta County Road 183, to discover the ghost town of Fayette in Fayette Historic State Park. Its history is rich in iron-smelting, dating back to when the town bustled in the late 1800s. Today, visitors flock to the area to soak in the peninsula's beautiful cliffs and harbors, and to explore historic buildings and experience a ghost town firsthand. Vineyards are cropping up on the peninsula, adding to the region's scenic beauty.

Drive north to Grand Marais, a quaint town located on Lake Superior and gateway to Pictured Rocks National Lakeshore. Nearby, the Grand Sables Dunes is a favorite challenge—just don't forget your sandals at the top before descending.

At Whitefish Point, just north of Paradise, find the Great Lakes Shipwreck Museum, where the bell of the Edmund Fitzgerald still rings once a year. Wrap up your day with a hike and overnight camping at Tahquamenon Falls.

A side trip to Hessel will take you to Katydid, an enchanting seasonal shop full of home décor, quality toys, and gifts. Sample wines produced by Black Star Farms, charmingly labeled with the large green long-horned grasshopper.

Your U.P. experience wouldn't be complete without dining on a fresh pasty, the region's homemade, healthy "fast-food" chock full of hearty meat, potatoes, and other veggies, reminiscent of Michigan's mining era.

Nicholas's Black River Vineyard and Winery

Red and gold kites dance in the bright azure sky along Mackinaw City's waterfront, which echoes with the sound of Lake Huron waves crashing ashore. Children spooning ice cream into their mouths and families trying their luck at the miniature golf course provide a perfect summertime backdrop as you stroll along Huron Street.

The call of seagulls flying overhead and the hum of ferryboats coming and going to Mackinac Island provide the beat as you head to the Mackinac Bay Trading Company, where you'll find the tasting room of Nicholas's Black River Vineyard and Winery.

The Mackinaw City tasting room is located within the cedar log-cabin building where you can stroll leisurely through the large gift shop and ask for a free sample of wine. Either Melacrinos sister, Maria or Alea, may be behind the tasting table pouring wines such as Ambrosia, distinguished for secret Greek spices and a touch of cinnamon. Don't miss tasting the Mighty Mac, a semidry red labeled with an image of Michigan's five-mile suspension bridge. Step outside to see the mighty Mackinac Bridge, viewable from the sidewalk that runs west-east along the Straits of Mackinac.

In tasting their wines, you may note a subtle difference. Alea differentiates their winery by their "light reds." Of their 11 wines, more than half are produced with red varietal grapes. "Our wines are very light—even our Merlot," says Maria. "We make our wines easy to drink and go down."

Demetrios and Alea in the vineyard.

The winery is the American dream of the sisters' maternal great-uncle, Nicholas Koklanaris. When Nicholas arrived in the United States from Ikaria, Greece, in 1951 he first enjoyed a career in construction. An injury resulted in his early retirement and in a need for a hobby to occupy his time.

As shared by Alea, "It is tradition for every household on Ikaria to make wine for family gatherings and special occasions." Nicholas was reminded of this and his grandfather's interest in wine and planted vines along the Black River in Cheboygan in 1992.

"Our great-uncle fondly recalled his grandfather working sunup to sundown sifting dirt, picking rocks, and preparing soil for grapevines," adds Alea. Before Nicholas passed away, younger sister Maria was invited to return to America to learn winemaking as her great-uncle's apprentice and future proprietor. Alea followed her sister soon after.

Although the Melacrinos sisters were born in Pittsburgh, they spent most of their life on Ikaria influenced by the Greek work ethic. With the help of their father, Demetrios, they run the full winery operation, from picking the grapes, winemaking, and bottling to serving the wines and providing vineyard tours.

If you make the countryside trip to the winery located seven miles south of Cheboygan, be on the lookout for a ranch-style house with a small building located behind it; the winery sign is visible from the road. Butler Road south of Cheboygan turns into Black River Road and the winery is on the right-hand side of the road.

Highlights of visiting the winery include the lovely 10-acre vineyard outlined by mammoth pines that tower over the Black River behind them. Most notably, though, appreciate the hand-painted murals in the winemaking room depicting Nicholas's journey to America on the north wall, the mythology of the island of Ikaria on the east wall, and the winemaking process on the south wall.

According to Alea, their family island, Ikaria, is named for the Greek mythology of Icaros, who is prominently featured in their winemaking room mural. Icaros, she shares, was the son of the inventor and architect Daedalus, who was locked into the labyrinth of Knossos after his father had helped Theseus defeat the Minotaur. Daedalus made two pairs of wings for himself and his son, made of feathers and wax to allow them to fly away from their prison. Despite his father's warnings, Icaros flew too near the sun. The wax then melted and the young man fell into the sea and drowned. Since then, the sea was called the Icarian Sea, and an island nearby called Ikaria.

At the Cheboygan winery, inquire about the wall murals and a vineyard tour, which the Melacrinos family can typically oblige.

During your visit to either location, you'll find customer favorite and gold medal winner Black River Red as well as the Ten Point, crafted by Nicholas to attract resident hunters; it's the family's only wine that features its own unique label. To wrap up your visit, you may wish to silently toast Nicholas for achieving the American dream with his namesake wine, Nick's Dry Red, a perfect ending to a northern Michigan day.

GET IN TOUCH:

6209 North Black River Road
Cheboygan
(231) 625-9060
www.nicholasblackriverwinery.com
GPS: N 45° 32.56698, W 084° 22.746

Tasting Room:
Mackinaw City
312 South Huron Avenue
(231) 436-5770
GPS: N 45° 46.78134, W 084° 43.5606

Parmenter's Northville Cider Mill Winery

Parmenter's Northville Cider Mill Winery has a rich history dating back 130-plus years. Four generations of Parmenters ran the mill for more than 90 years before making the tough decision to sell. Northville's second-oldest business, though, continues to thrive as an autumn-only destination for families in the region. Get your fall cider and Michigan wine, too, at this fun, family-run gem by the Rouge River.

The history of the mill starts in 1873 as a vinegar company owned by Benijah A. Parmenter, who operated the business until his death in 1921. His son William continued the mill until his death in 1948, when his son Harold (called "Cider") began running the mill. Later Harold's son Robert took over and continued the mill until 1967.

Current owners Diane and Mel Jones and Cheryl and Rob Nelson bought the mill from a subsequent owner in 1991, adding a winery the year after to expand their product line. They produce a hard cider, as well as three wines: Niagara, a sweet, white wine; Just White, a dry blend of Seyval Blanc and Vignoles; and Michigan Red, a fruity blend of De Chaunac and Maréchal Foch. "Our semidry Michigan Red is a little sweeter than a Merlot," describes Diane.

Parmenter's is also a great place to enjoy apple cider and donuts as well as freshly made caramel apples and apple pies, homemade fudge, apple butter, maple syrup, Brownwood jam, vinegar, honey, summer sausage, salsa, lollipops, and more. Diane shares with us that, "The majority of products are Michigan-made."

Get your fall cider and Michigan wine, too, at this fun, family-run gem by the Rouge River.

Stop by the Fudge Hut for some homemade fudge or the Nut Mill for fresh cinnamon-roasted almonds and cinnamon-roasted pecans. Larger appetites can be satiated at the Chow Mill, offering hot dogs, kielbasa, sauerkraut, chips, and cider by the glass. On golden fall days, rather than eat indoors, head down to the river and sit on a bench or spread out on the picnic tables. "We're on the middle fork of the Rouge River. Children enjoy feeding the ducks," says Diane. We're sure your family will make this cider mill a favorite destination for repeat visits every autumn.

GET IN TOUCH

714 Baseline Road
Northville
(248) 349-3181
info@northvillecider.com
www.northvillecider.com
GPS: N 42° 26.25378, W 083° 28.42962

Pleasantview Vineyards

Staking new winemaking territory in northwest Michigan, further north of Michigan's peninsula wine trails, is Pleasantview Vineyards. Husband and wife team Dr. Jerry Perrone and Sandy Pfister are pros at hospitality, as they have been operating Highland Hideaway Bed and Breakfast Resort for more than 15 years, near popular ski and golf resorts Boyne Highlands and Nub's Nob.

"I was just getting back from Saudi Arabia, nearing retirement when we began looking for property for a bed-and-breakfast. I told Sandy, 'you see something you like, buy it.' We've traveled all over the world. She knows what we want. She looked at all the big resort areas, like Park City. We just love it up here," says Jerry.

Sandy's family history is deeply entrenched in this region and up into the Upper Peninsula. Over a glass of wine, indulge in relaxation and ask Sandy about her most-unique cultural heritage. You'll learn of her great-great-great-great-grandfather, a "swash-buckling privateer" in the late 1700s and early 1800s, who was given a land grant in this region by the Queen of England. The privateer never made it to the New World, but his daughter later established fur trading with the Native Americans and several towns in the U.P.

More than a century later, Sandy's most beloved grandfather worked the coal mines in Copper Harbor until his death. Photographs of the bygone era and industry hang in Sandy and Jerry's Sunset House Bed and Breakfast.

The bed-and-breakfast is just one of several buildings on their six acres in Harbor Springs' beautiful countryside. Most recently, the "retired" entrepreneurs opened a tasting room to promote wines Jerry has been producing for years. "I've always been winemaking. My family has been making wine for years in California. It's always been part of my life."

The retired marine now spends his days experimenting and crafting wines with his Valiant, Niagara, and Edelweiss grapes, which he shares, "grow really well here." He also uses Concord grapes from Charlevoix and Delaware grapes from Cheboygan, all within proximity to their homestead.

"Our inn guests have made great informal testers," laughs Sandy. Encouraged by their customers to officially open a winery, the couple did just that with their Pleasantview Vineyards in 2006. Surrounded by a forest of trees on an impressive hillside, their resort also includes the Sauterne House vacation rental.

Stop by and visit Jerry and Sandy and ring the bell when you arrive. They may be at their bed-and-breakfast entertaining guests on the expansive back patio. When they hear the ring, they'll rush over to give you a taste of their wine selection, which now also includes an ice wine called Frost. Jerry is sure to share tips on how to get the most enjoyment out of a glass of his wine.

Wines crafted on their property include Crystal Harmony, a clean, crisp white wine. Lisse Oro is described as "rich with flavor and character." Their

Sunglow rosé is subtly sweet, while their more full-bodied red wine, Cottage Bistro, is crafted for those who prefer their reds more complex. Sandy shares that they may produce a wine using the wild grapes grown throughout northern Michigan. We're looking forward to trying it, as we grew up with wild grapes weaving through our backyards.

An elaborate dove house behind the winery is home to white doves the owners provide for weddings and funerals. "They're big hams; they know their part well," Jerry surprisingly shares. The doves provide a serene beauty to special events, which Jerry and Sandy often host on-site in their conservatory.

This tucked-away gem is worth a visit to experience wines from one of Michigan's newest growing regions, and to kick back with a glass of wine and listen to swashbuckling adventures.

"Our inn guests have made great informal testers".

GET IN TOUCH

6769 South Pleasantview Road
Harbor Springs
(231) 526-8100
pleasantviewvineyards@yahoo.com
www.pleasantviewwinery.us
GPS: N 45° 27.2322, W 084° 54.88476

Robinette Cellars

Cherry picking was in full swing when we caught up with hard cider brew-master Bill Robinette and younger brother John in the family's orchards full of plump-for-the-picking sweet, tart, and black cherries.

John was getting customers started with empty buckets from the Cherry Hut, while Bill, his hands already cherry-stained from his task, was filling up tubs to take back to the Apple Haus for customers who preferred their cherries already plucked. The late Barzilla Robinette, great-grandfather to the boys and oldest brother Ed, would have been proud to see his U-Pick farm bustling with happy customers and his great-grandchildren carrying on the family legacy.

The Robinette farm is amazingly preserved and surrounded by trees, orchards, and county park land on 125 acres off busy East Beltline Avenue and Four Mile Road in Grand Rapids. You'd never know the farm existed—as it has for nearly 140 years—nor would you expect to find the spacious farm and gracious hospitality of the Robinette clan, led by Ed's delightful, charming wife, Alicia, just off the interstate.

The Robinette's history on the farm gets started when Barzilla Robinette bought the farm in 1911. His oldest son, Edward, gave up his teaching career to manage the day-to-day needs of the farm. Back then, the Robinettes grew everything from hogs to melons and established orchards of peaches, apples, and cherries. When a shortage of labor occurred during World War II, Edward pioneered "pick your own cherries," which is very much alive today on the working farm.

The Robinette story continues with Edward's son James and wife Bethel running the family's wholesale operation until 1971, when customer demand for apples prompted them to open the cider mill. In 1973, they built a wood-beam Apple Haus with a soaring, two-story peaked roof to store 12,000 bushels of apples at 34 degrees behind tall vaulted doors. In season, request a peek into the massive apple storage where you can taste apples fresh behind the door. We're sure you'll take home a bag full after finding a favorite apple from their selection of 24 varieties.

The Apple Haus is loaded with fresh fruits of the season—cherries plucked fresh from the orchard; peaches, apricots, nectarines, pumpkins, and, of course, apples. Jams and jellies, apple syrup, and apple and pumpkin butter brighten up stacked shelves. Fresh baked goods—breads, pies, and pastries—are whipped up daily in the adjoining bakery, which Bethel initiated when the Apple Haus was first built.

Today, you can feast on homemade soups and sandwiches, or try a sample of delicious homemade fudge made by Karey Robinette, John's wife, who likes to experiment with new flavors. During fall and winter months, you may just catch sight of a fresh batch of apple cider being made through large, open windows within the Apple Haus. "You can hear it and see it," explains Ed.

Take your lunch tray outside on warm, sunny days and sit under the large maple trees next to the giant, 10-foot-tall apple made of urethane and covered with fiberglass in James and Bethel's front yard.

John and Bill during U-pick cherry season.

James and Bethel retired in the 1990s and still reside in the farmhouse, originally built by the farm's first owner in 1884.

The fourth generation of Robinettes brings you their family's newest venture: Michigan wine and hard apple cider, brewed by Bill on the Robinette farm. To get to the tasting bar, stroll through bright displays of gifts, home décor, and unique treasures within the Gift Barn, originally built in 1881 for horses and cows and renovated in 1985. In fact, we're told by Ed that when you taste wines in the barn's cellar, you'll be pretty close to where the horses hung their heads at night until about the 1920s. The original stone foundation provides the backdrop to where wines are poured while the original hand-hewed oak beams hang overhead.

out the door quickly. You might also be tempted to try their pear wine, an ideal accompaniment to chicken or pork. And their blend of five apples in their dessert apple wine tastes just like "a really good slice of apple pie," shares Marilyn Quigley, who was working behind the tasting bar the day we visited.

Cap off your visit with a hayride pulled by a team of beautiful Belgian horses, or, depending on the season, hike, mountain bike, or cross-country ski on rolling terrain within the 40-acre Provin Trails Park that borders the property to the west. The family extends a warm welcome to visit them any day of the year, whatever the season. In honor of the Robinette's history and centennial farm recognition, be sure to also celebrate with them in 2011—but don't wait that long to meet the friendly Robinette clan and enjoy their abundant fruit.

Barzilla's Brew is clear hard apple cider, with only six percent alcohol, made from apples picked especially for its creation. As a tribute to his great-grandfather, Bill named the brew for him. "It's a natural extension to our apple tradition," states Bill. Of course, we were curious about Barzilla's name and inquired if there was a story behind it. Bill shared that Barzilla is from the Bible, 2 Samuel 19: verses 31–39.

The wine selection also includes red and white table wines, Robin White, a blend of Riesling, Pinot Gris, and Pinot Blanc, and Robin Red, which goes down like a light Shiraz. Their best-selling cherry wine goes

GET IN TOUCH

3142 4 Mile Road NE
Grand Rapids
(800) 400-8100
bigapple@robinettes.com
www.robinettes.com
GPS: N 43° 1.67976, W 085° 35.4996

Stoney Acres Winery

Opening a winery wasn't always the plan for Helen Grochowski, unlike her husband and winemaker, James Grochowski. James, a hobby winemaker for more than 40 years, had much bigger ideas. "He bugged me for a good five years until I finally said yes, and that was only because I wanted to be able to get to my washer and dryer again by getting all the wine out of the way," laughs Helen.

James, who was quickly approaching retirement, knew he wouldn't be able to sit still as a retiree. Winemaking was a passion of his ever since he helped his grandfather craft wines as a little tyke. "James had been making wines since before we were married in 1966," recalls Helen.

The Grochowskis started the small, boutique winery in 1999 with modest goals, as Helen shares, "We started extremely small, about 200 gallons per year. Our goal was 10,000 gallons in 10 years, which we hit in only six years." The winery is truly a family undertaking. "I'm on the grunt force, day-to-day operations," explains Helen. "Jim is the winemaker, and our daughter, Amy, is a jack-of-all-trades."

Stoney Acres Winery, located on the state's sunrise side in Alpena, was named in honor of the acres of land covered with stone on which the property is located. "There are stones and stones and stones and boulders and boulders. We've used the stones every-where. We have stone retaining walls and a beautiful stone bar in the tasting room," describes Helen.

Inside the tasting room, make your way to the cobblestone bar to sample wines crafted by James from locally grown fruit including cranberry, blueberry, pear, strawberry, raspberry, apple, black sweet cherry, and blackberry, as well as some traditional grape wines. "All of our wines are made from the actual fruit," shares Helen.

Be sure to try their signature grape wines including Thunder Bay Red, a pale red wine made from Concord; Silver City White, a fruity wine made from Riesling; and Silver City Red, a deep red wine made from Merlot. Another good choice is their most popular Pear wine, a crisp white wine with a pure glowing blend of pears.

A sampling not to miss is their Raspberry, Strawberry, or Cherry served with a delectable piece of chocolate. "The chocolate is often walked out with the wine, as well as supplies for making beer and wine at home," shares Helen.

Enjoy a sip of wine on their large outdoor patio, surrounded by beautiful fencing separated by pillars—made of cobblestone, of course—or take a walk through the countryside as Helen invites you to, "Meander around and enjoy nature."

GET IN TOUCH

4268 Truckey Road
Alpena
(989) 356-1041
GPS: N 45° 6.52158, W 083° 28.59108

Tartan Hill Winery

Off the beaten path is Tartan Hill Winery, a lovely vineyard and winery with, what we're told, the best sunset views. The evening sun appears to light up the treetops surrounding the vineyard every cloudless evening. When you visit at daylight, pause a moment to take in the beautiful countryside setting that surrounds you before walking through an archway of grapevines into the rustic tasting room.

Tartan Hill Winery is located in Oceana County on Michigan's "left coast," midway off U.S. 31 in New Era, about 50 miles north of Grand Rapids. You may be surprised to learn that this county holds the second largest fruit tree acreage in the state and it's "the asparagus capital of the world." Besides fruit and veggies, you'll be close to one of the few places in the nation offering dune schooner rides—along sandy Lake Michigan in Silver Lake, along the road a few miles.

The county's only winery was established in 1985 getting its name in honor of the original proprietors', Bob and Carol Cameron's, Scottish heritage. Since then, the winery changed hands to Paul and Beverly Goralski, who run the winery along with son and winemaker Greg and daughter-in-law Renae.

Greg crafts their 100 percent, estate-bottled wines, blending varieties from different vintages. "Most of our wines are made from blending grapes," Renae shares. "Since we only use fruit grown in our vineyard, production is somewhat limited." A favorite of Renae's is the Cayuga Jazz, which is produced with Cayuga grapes and blended with a touch of raspberries.

Renae says that the winery's location a few miles inland from Lake Michigan on high terrain is ideal for growing grapes. When we visited, their eight acres of vines came alive in the summer breeze; vines full of healthy leaves danced above lavender that we were tempted to make a bouquet of for its heavenly scent.

Our stop at Tartan Hall was a lovely respite along Michigan's beautiful western shores. Someday soon, we hope to catch one of their sunsets over a glass of Cayuga Jazz.

Our stop at Tartan Hall was a lovely respite along Michigan's beautiful western shores.

Renae also recommends chilling the Oceana Piper's Red, a semisweet red wine blend that is primarily made with Maréchal Foch grapes. "It's a very nice wine; we recommend this to our customers whose doctors have suggested they drink red wine for its health benefits," expresses Renae.

For dryer taste buds, try the Dry Seyval, which Renae touts as a "nice blending of whites with pear aroma" and the Proprietor's Reserve Red with a rich, scarlet color and Hungarian oak aroma. Renae describes it as "soft and smoky" and also recommends letting it breathe in a decanter to fully appreciate its flavors.

GET IN TOUCH

4937 South 52nd Avenue
New Era
(231) 861-4657
info@tartanhillwinery.com
www.tartanhillwinery.com
GPS: N 43° 33.38376, W 086° 25.66842

Threefold Vine Winery

Threefold Vine Winery was established in the Upper Peninsula in 2006 on a massive 470-acre farm in the village of Garden, named for the fertility of its soil. Thirty different grape varieties cover four acres with "five to six varieties showing great promise," says proprietor Andrew Green. "We plan to use only the grapes we grow here on our farm and utilize as many organic practices as are practical for us in the vineyard, orchards, and all our farming." Fruit grown in their orchards and honey from their family bees are used in making their wines.

Janice, Andrew's wife and coproprietor, shares, "We're offering apple and honey wines and also a cherry and raspberry dessert wine." They plan to expand their selection of wines as their grapevines mature. Visit the Greens on your next adventure to the U.P.

GET IN TOUCH

5856 NN Road
Garden
(906) 644-7089
threefoldvine@hotmail.com
www.exploringthenorth.com/
 threefold/vine.html
GPS: N 45° 44.92938, W 086° 33.84006

Wyncroft

Wyncroft specializes in high-quality, high-end wines available only by the case through an exclusive mailing list, or by the bottle at an impressive list of upscale restaurants across the state. It was the love for food and the desire to complement the fare with the right wines that landed Jim and Rae Lee Lester in the art of winemaking.

Over the years, Jim and Rae Lee savored delicious gourmet foods, most often prepared by Rae Lee. As Rae Lee honed her cooking skills, they read, studied, and experimented with wine to get the perfect match. The more they learned, the more they fell in love with wine and eventually wanted to craft their own perfect wines to match the fare. "We couldn't afford our own palate," chuckles Jim.

Jim and Rae Lee only grow varieties that are right for their growing conditions and only varieties they believe are the best in the world to consistently craft wines to their standards. "We have the maritime climate because we are right at the bottom of the lake," explains Jim.

Two vineyards, Madron Lake Vineyard and Avonlea Vineyard, host the grapevines from which their wine is produced. Madron Lake Vineyard holds five acres of Riesling and a third of an acre of Gewürztraminer. Avonlea Vineyard holds ten acres, with about five acres of Chardonnay, half an acre of Riesling, an acre of Pinot Noir, and the rest with Cabernet Sauvignon, Merlot, and Cabernet Franc.

Jim also takes the time to protect his vines from the birds, "I use a rifle to scare the birds. I shoot for three or four hours early every morning right before harvest to keep the flocks of starlings away. If I don't, they'll make great work of eating all of our grapes."

Jim and Rae Lee craft the wines by hand every step of the way, taking their time to age the wines in oak barrels to the perfect bottling moment. "We try to get the most out of the fruit without chemical manipulation," Jim explains. "Our goal is to produce French-style boutique wine, so we only use French yeast, and we want to produce the best dry red wine you can buy anywhere."

You'll need to decide for yourself how Wyncroft's wines rate, as Jim will tell you, "We don't enter our wines in competitions. We're really not interested in winning awards, but our wines seem to end up in blind tastings from loyal customers who take them there, and they always seem to blow people away."

As with the entire winemaking process, Jim and Rae Lee take the sampling of their wines very seriously as well. You can set up a private wine tasting with the Lesters, who will spend as much time with you as you desire to experience their wines. "We like to personally know the people who buy our wines," shares Jim.

You can purchase their wines during a private tasting or by joining their exclusive mailing list, where you will be informed about new releases along with information about the vintage, the winemaking process, how to cellar the wine, and the best foods to pair it with. You can also visit their web site for the list of restaurants where you may be able to enjoy a bottle of one of Wyncroft's premium wines.

GET IN TOUCH

716-B East Front Street
Buchanan
(269) 695-8000
wyncroft@sbcglobal.net
www.wyncroftwine.com
GPS: N 41° 49.64148, W 086° 21.6582

The Trail Ahead

Good news for Michigan! With plans for a number of new wineries to open within the next few years, you will have even more opportunities to explore Michigan wine trails and beyond the trails into Michigan's many glorious nooks. The more than 50 wineries will give you plenty of options for stocking up your informal or refined wine cellars—without even leaving our Great Lakes state.

Before visiting any winery, be sure to visit their web sites for seasonal hours, as many wineries shorten their hours during winter months; some wineries even close from late fall to early spring.

Please note, too, that as we heard quite often along our journey, it takes substantial time and capital commitments to start up a winery and plant a vineyard. There may be times when, unfortunately, one of the wineries closes its doors. Most of Michigan's wineries are small businesses with huge investments in their wines. Support them as you would any local business to keep them prosperous.

We have worked very hard to ensure the information within our book is accurate; however, please note that you may find errors, which are ours alone. As shared in our introduction, we are not wine experts—not by a long shot. We are advocates for Michigan, its wines and its farmers, entrepreneurs, and conservationists.

Acknowledgments

Our book would not be on bookshelves and in tasting rooms without the unwavering support of our husbands, John Hathaway and Kris Kegerreis, and our children: Anthony, Capri, Calli and Jack, and Julia and Makayla, respectively.

Thank you, too, to our parents: Linda and the late Bob Ihme of Glen Arbor and Richard and Margaret Martin of Charlevoix, for their constant encouragement and obvious skills at grooming us to be responsible wine enthusiasts and for chucking big city life to raise us in two of northern Michigan's most beautiful tourism communities, Leelanau Peninsula and Charlevoix.

A huge thanks to go-to, talented photographer, Michael Crain, and sit-in interviewer and Sharon's sister Anastasia Crain, for trekking into the U.P. and wherever else we needed photographs. The experiences you shared polished a handful of stories.

Thank you, Linda Ihme and Kelly Ciolek, Lorri's sister; Anastasia Crain, and Dave and Toni Worley for their feedback on our work in progress.

Thank you, Mark and Kristen Shuert, for jumping to our rescue when we called in need of photographers who could capture our personalities on film … er, in megapixels.

Thank you to Margaret Martin and Jennifer Sinkwitts for extra writing days, and Heather Cavin, who dropped everything and came to the rescue on book delivery day.

Thank you, Amanda Gougeon, our intern, for your fact finding and research skills.

Thank you to Linda Jones, Karel Bush, and David Creighton of Michigan Grape and Wine Council for their overall support in our quest to spread the word about Michigan wines, and for use of their digital maps as our base maps.

We especially wish to thank the vintners who took time out of their busy days, many during harvest, to meet with us, share their stories, and give us incredible insight into the art of winemaking. They posed for us, took us to their favorite vineyard views, and gave us early tastes of their yet-to-be released wines. It's an honor for us to tell your stories. It was your wines we sipped late at night that encouraged us to keep writing.

Most of all, thank you for reading our stories. We hope you've enjoyed meeting the creative people behind Michigan wine in our pages. Visit their tasting rooms today, and we're sure you'll find many Michigan wines to take home with you.

A special thank you to Michigan Grape and Wine Industry Council for the base maps. Visit them online at: www.michiganwines.com.

Glossary

ageing: All wine is aged, from a few weeks to many decades. Ageing in barrels is a very slow oxidation, and the barrels can impart flavors to the wine. Bottle ageing allows the wines to soften and various components within the wine to harmonize; though, after a certain point, all wine will decline in the bottle.

Alsace: a region in France known for producing high-quality white wines with a strong German influence, such as Riesling.

aperitif: any wine served before or after a meal.

aroma: a term loosely used to describe the smell of wine, specifically as it refers to the smells that derive from grapes. It is now also used to describe a wine's complete smell, including from oak ageing.

Aurore: a French hybrid table grape or wine grape used for a range of white wine styles including dry, off-dry, and sparkling.

Auxerrois: a red wine grape variety (also the local French name for the Malbec) grown in the Cahors region of France.

Auxerrois Blanc: a white wine grape primarily grown in France's Alsace region and used to produce wine that is crisp, dry white with spicy apple and citrus aromas.

Baco Noir: a French hybrid grape used to produce a medium body, deeply tinted, acidic red wine that is fruit forward and carries aromas of vanilla and chocolate.

Balaton®: a cherry variety excellent for processing with its red skin, flesh, and juice; while its vibrant color makes it especially appealing.

Bordeaux: a region in southwest France considered by most as the world's greatest wine-producing region because of the large quantity and the high quality of the wines.

bouquet: a tasting term used to describe the smell of the wine as it matures in the bottle.

breathe: allowing a bottle of wine to stand for several minutes (to several hours) after the cork is removed, but before serving, as it is believed that wines improve by air exposure prior to serving.

brut: French for dry.

Cabernet Franc: a red wine grape variety similar to Cabernet Sauvignon and best suited for colder climate regions. It's used to produce red wines with aromas such as herbaceousness and a pronounced peppery nose and light tobacco.

Cabernet Sauvignon: a variety of red grape with a thick skin resulting in the popular red wine; generally full flavored with a smooth and lingering finish that also ages well.

Cayuga White: a hardy hybrid grape variety best suited for cold climates with some disease resistance. It produces a very nice sparkling wine with good acid balance, structure, and pleasant aromas or a fruity white wine similar to a Riesling.

Chambourcin: a red French-American hybrid grape variety that produces a deep-colored wine with a full aromatic flavor and no unpleasant hybrid flavors.

Chancellor: a red French-American hybrid widely grown in the Eastern United States that produces fruity, slightly blander red wines.

Chardonnay: a green-skinned grape variety used to make a popular white wine that, when aged with oak, can acquire smoky, vanilla, caramel, and butter aromas.

Chelois: a red hybrid grape with small blue-black berries that appear in compact, medium-sized clusters.

Chenin Blanc: a naturally hard, acidic grape, slow to mature, that is usually made into fine sweet wines that age well for at least ten years in the bottle.

Concord: a grape used both as table grapes and wine grapes that typically has a dark blue or purple skin that is easily separated from the fruit. Concord grapes have large seeds and are highly aromatic.

cuvée: From the French cuve ("vat"), and referring to the "contents of a vat." In the Champagne region of France, the word refers to a blended batch of wines.

cuve close method: a bulk method for making sparkling wines using large vats or tanks that retain the pressure created during a second fermentation.

De Chaunac: a French-American hybrid grape used to make red wines and known to have a very vigorous growth habit and good resistance to powdery mildew and downy mildew.

Delaware: a Native American hybrid grape widely used in the production of everything from dry to sweet and sparkling white wines of good quality, often with spicy aromas.

Dolcetto: a red wine grape, whose name translates to "little sweet one," that is grown mainly in the southwest section of Italy's Piedmont region. Dolcetto wines have high acidity, are usually deep purple in color, and have perfumy bouquets and rich, fruity, ripe-berry flavors, sometimes with a slightly bitter aftertaste.

Edelweiss: a very winter-hardy grape used as a table grape or wine grape that produces a green-to-amber-colored, early-ripening, fruit.

eiswein (ice wine): a German term meaning "ice wine," referring to a rich, flavorful dessert wine.

Fennville (AVA): Michigan's first AVA as established in 1981, whose eastern boundary borders a state game reserve, with the remaining natural boundaries being Lake Michigan to the west, the Kalamazoo River to the north, and the Black River to the south.

fermentation: a natural process that turns grape juice into wine; fermentation is actually a chain reaction of chemical responses and typically refers to the conversion of sugar to alcohol using yeast. However, a more appropriate definition would be the chemical conversion of carbohydrates into alcohols or acids.

Frontenac: a grape variety that is cold-hardy and very resistant to disease, used to produce wines that are usually deeply colored with a pleasing cherry aroma, and with plum and berry often evident.

Gamay Noir: a purple-colored grape used to make red wines and probably originally a mutation of Pinot Noir.

Gewürztraminer: a white wine grape that performs best in cooler climates, known for its spicy characteristics and strong smell of lychees on the bouquet, believed to be related to Viognier.

hybrid: a cross between two species of a grapevine that tend to be less susceptible to frost and disease.

La Crescent: a tough and cold-hardy grape varietal successful in producing sweet white wines and often used as a component of blends.

La Crosse: a cold-hardy hybrid grape capable of making good-quality, fruity white wines.

Lake Michigan Shore (AVA): Michigan's largest AVA with broad boundaries, which include the smaller Fennville appellation, extending as far as 45 miles inland from the lakeshore and 70 miles from the Indiana border to the Kalamazoo River at Saugatuck.

late harvest: wines made from grapes allowed to hang on the vine longer until sugar content is very high, resulting in sweeter wine.

Leelanau Peninsula (AVA): an AVA geographically consisting of the Leelanau Peninsula with its finger-like projections extending into Lake Michigan at Grand Traverse Bay.

Lemberger: a wine grape that is used to produce dry, red wines that are typically low in tannin and may exhibit a pronounced spicy character.

Malbec: a black, mellow grape that creates a rather inky red (or violet), intense wine; it is also commonly used in blends.

Maréchal Foch: a French-American hybrid grown widely in Michigan and used for semisweet blush wines with a deep-red, almost black color and low tannin.

Marsanne: a not-so-common grape used to create wines that are rich and nutty, with hints of spice and pear or, when grown in Australia, aromas of melon and honeysuckle.

melange: a mixture or, in wine terms, a blending of flavors.

Merlot: one of the noble wine grape varieties, used to create a popular red wine usually with a medium body and hints of berry, plum, and currant.

méthode Champenoise: the traditional method of making sparkling wine developed in France's Champagne region. This process consists of taking various still wines and blending them to make a cuvée. After the wines are blended, special yeasts are added, and the cuvée is immediately bottled and corked. The yeast and sugar in the dosage create a secondary fermentation in the bottle, producing additional alcohol and carbon dioxide gas, which gives the wine its effervescence.

Muscat: a grape used for winemaking, table grapes, and raisins that comprise hundreds of varieties ranging in color from white to almost black. Muscat wines are noted for their musky, fresh-grape flavors and range from fine, light whites (often sparkling) to sweet, dark versions (often fortified).

Niagara: the leading green grape grown in the United States used to make wines, as well as jams and juice. The fresh grape is large and juicy, round to oval-shaped, pale greenish-white in color, and has a sweet, very pleasant aroma.

Old Mission Peninsula (AVA): Michigan's fourth AVA, consisting of the Old Mission Peninsula, a fingerlike piece of land that juts 19 miles northward from Traverse City into Grand Traverse Bay, splitting the bay into a western and an eastern arm with only three miles of land at its widest.

Petite Sirah: a red wine grape that produces a deep-colored, robust, and peppery wine that packs plenty of tannins and has good ageing ability.

Petit Verdot: a black grape used in the production of red wine, principally in blends with Cabernet Sauvignon, to add aroma, color, acid, and tannin with a good mid-palate character.

Pinot Blanc: a white wine grape known for its uncomplicated, mildly flavored wines, which can often be refreshingly tart from cool growing regions.

Pinot Meunier: a variety of black wine grape most frequently used in the production of Champagne, but can also make an enjoyable dry red wine, like a more fruity and rustic Pinot Noir.

Pinot Noir: a red wine grape with a tremendously broad range of bouquets, flavors, textures, and impressions used to produce wines that tend to be of light to medium body with an aroma reminiscent of black cherry, raspberry, or currant.

port: a fortified wine that is very richly flavored and sweet.

Regent: an inter-specific French-American red hybrid grape used for making wine. It supplies color-intensive strong red wines and is well-known in German wine regions.

residual sugar: the amount of sugar left in wine at bottling.

Rhône: a wine region in France known for producing high-quality wines divided into north and south: the north produces Syrah-based reds and pure Viognier whites. The south produces Châteauneuf-du-Pape and other blends from several varieties.

Rhine: a renowned wine region of Germany known for producing quality wines.

Riesling: a white grape variety and varietal appellation of wines grown historically in Alsace (France), Austria, Germany, and northern Italy, but becoming increasingly popular in Michigan.

St. Croix: a cold-hardy grape that produces sweet bluish-red fruit used both as a table grape and for producing wine.

St. Pepin: a cold-hardy grape used to produce both juices and wines.

Sauvignon Blanc: a white wine grape that produces wines with noticeable acidity and a grassy, herbaceous aroma and flavor. These are crisp, flavorful wines that should be drunk young.

Seyval: a popular French-American hybrid grape used to make crisp white wines or sometimes off-dry versions where the tart nature of the variety is balanced with residual sugar.

sherry: a fortified wine ranging from dry to very sweet, from amber to brown in color.

solera: a method of blending sherries. The first sherry is "laid down" in a cask. The next year, a similar tasting sherry is put above it. Some sherry is taken from the bottom cask, and it is "replenished" with liquid from the cask over it, which is replenished from the cask over it, and so on. Only 33 percent of the solera is removed per year, maintaining a consistent sherry taste.

spumante: Italian for "sparkling," "foamy," or "frothy," referring to fully sparkling wines, as opposed to those that are slightly sparkling (frizzante).

Syrah/Shiraz: a grape variety widely used to make a dry red table wine, often vinified on its own, but is also frequently blended with other grape varieties. Australians refer to this grape as "Shiraz."

tannin: any of a group of astringent substances found in the seeds, skins, and stems of grapes, as well as in oak barrels, particularly new ones.

terroir: French for earth or soil, used in the special sense of "place," which includes localized climate, soil type, drainage, wind direction, humidity, and all the other attributes that combine to make one location different from another.

Traminette: a French-American hybrid found to have excellent wine quality, combined with good productivity, partial resistance to several fungal diseases, and cold hardiness superior to its acclaimed parent, Gewürztraminer, while retaining a similar character.

Upper Peninsula: the northern portion of Michigan's two land masses, accessible via the Mackinac Bridge from Michigan's Lower Peninsula. The Upper Peninsula is bordered by Canada, Lake Superior, Lake Huron, Lake Michigan, and Wisconsin.

Valiant: a cold-hardy grape variety used as table grapes and to make jelly as well as red wine, mostly as a blend with other varieties.

value-added agriculture: a process of increasing the economic value and consumer appeal of an agricultural commodity; discovering and marketing new strategies for promoting a food product.

varietal: a wine that uses the name of the dominant grape from which it's made, such as Cabernet Sauvignon, Chardonnay, and Riesling.

Vidal Blanc: an inter-specific hybrid variety of white wine grape that produces high sugar levels in cold climates while maintaining good acid levels to produce wines that are fruity, with grapefruit and pineapple notes, particularly sweeter dessert wines.

Vignoles: a complex hybrid wine grape variety that makes a wine with a sweet and flowery bouquet and a clean, crisp, sweet pineapple flavor balanced with agreeable acidity.

Vinifera: vine species that produces over 99 percent of the world's wines today. It is native to Europe, but it has been planted all over the world.

vintage: a single specified year in which wine is made from grapes that were all, or primarily, grown.

vintner: wine producer or winery proprietor.

viticulture: The science and art of grape growing, as distinguished from viniculture, the science of winemaking.

Viognier: a white wine grape used to produce a wine whose color and floral aroma suggest a sweet wine but are predominantly dry, although sweet late harvest dessert wines are also made.

Yeast: promotes fermentation of grape juice. The "dust" on a grape, known as the "bloom," is wild yeast.

Bibliography

Charter, Kay, "Vineyard is ripe for bird viewing," *Traverse City Record Eagle*, September 10, 2006.

South, Carol, "Winery habitat for the bird; bird group honors Chateau Grand Traverse for its efforts," *Traverse City Record Eagle*, July 19, 2006.

Stevenson, Tom, *Sotheby's Wine Encyclopedia: The Classic Reference to Wines of the World*, DK Publishing, 2005.

Stevenson, Tom, *Wine Report 2007*, DK Publishing, 2006.

"Award-Winning Michigan Wines 2005–2006," Michigan Grape and Wine Industry Council. www.michiganwines.com/Awards.

"News and Events," Wine Appreciation Guild. www.wineappreciation.com.

"Pinot Meunier," Appellation America. wine.appellationamerica.com/grape-varietal/Pinot-Meunier.

Center for Wine Origins. www.wineorigins.com.

Wikipedia, The Free Encyclopedia, 2006.

Wikipediaen.wikipedia.org/wiki/Frizzante.

Wine Reference Resource. www.cellarnotes.net.

www.answers.com/Spumante

www.gpsvisualizer.com

www.msu.edu

www.wineintro.com

www.wine.com

Glossary Definitions

www.appellationamerica.com

www.epicurious.com

www.michiganbalatoncherries.com

www.thewineman.com/glossary

www.wikipedia.com

Photo Credits

All photos were taken by the authors except for the following:

Cover photo Brian Confer

P. 14 (truffle), 23, 83, 90 (steps), 92, 122, 162, 163, 164, 165, 172 Michael Crain

P. 20, 21 Courtesy of Fenn Valley Vineyards

P. 39 Kristopher Kegerreis

P. 49 Gregg Rizzo, Tabor Hill Winery

P. 55 Joshua Maurer, The Technology Works (www.yourtechworks.com)

P. 61 (Inn) William Kennedy

P. 76 Margie Araquistain, Cherry Republic

P. 78 (Ciccones) Cindy K. Hughes Photography (www.ckhughes.com)

P. 128 Eddie O'Keefe III, Chateau Grand Traverse

P. 161 Joni Smoker, Krolczyk Cellars

P. 177 Amy Gagnon, Stoney Acres Winery

P. 181 Andrew Green, Threefold Vine Winery

P. 182, 183 Trevor Rudderham (www.thevarietyoflight.com)

P. 184, authors' photo Kristen Shuert